REACHING
HIGHER

TWENTY-FIVE WAYS
TO FEEL BETTER
ABOUT YOURSELF

REACHING HIGHER

TWENTY-FIVE WAYS
TO FEEL BETTER
ABOUT YOURSELF

Steven A. Cramer

CFI
Springville, Utah

ISBN 13: 978-1-59955-122-7

Published by CFI, an imprint of Cedar Fort, Inc., 2373 W. 700 S., Springville, UT, 84663
Distributed by Cedar Fort, Inc., www.cedarfort.com

LIBRARY OF CONGRESS CATALOGING-IN-PUBLICATION DATA

Cramer, Steven A.
  [Draw near unto me]
  Reaching higher : twenty-five ways to feel better about yourself / Steven
A. Cramer.
    p. cm.
  Originally published: Draw near unto me. American Fork, UT: Covenant
Communications, 2001.
  ISBN 978-1-59955-122-7
  1. Christian life—Mormon authors—Miscellanea. 2. Church of Jesus Christ
of Latter-day Saints—Doctrines—Miscellanea. I. Title.

  BX8656.C734 2007
  248.4'89332—dc22

                    2007045098

Cover design by Nicole Williams
Cover design © 2008 by Lyle Mortimer
Edited and typeset by Annaliese B. Cox

Printed in the United States of America

10 9 8 7 6 5 4 3 2 1

Printed on acid-free paper

And ye cannot bear all things now; nevertheless, be of good cheer, for I will lead you along. The kingdom is yours and the blessings thereof are yours, and the riches of eternity are yours.

—*D&C 78:18*

ALSO BY STEVEN A. CRAMER

Chosen
Conquering Your Own Goliaths
Great Shall Be Your Joy
In the Arms of His Love
Putting on the Armor of God
The Worth of a Soul
The Worth of Every Soul
Victory in Christ

CONTENTS

CONTENTS

INTRODUCTION

DID YOU KNOW the scriptures contain over 4,000 questions?

I just asked you a question! I could have just *told* you: The scriptures contain over 4,000 questions.

Which would you have preferred, that I *told* you how many questions there are, or that I *asked*? (Whoops, there's another question.)

Most people feel that questions are more thought-provoking and interesting than mere dissertation. In fact, the definition of a question is "an expression of inquiry *that invites or calls for a response.*"

Most of the questions considered in this work were asked by the Lord, challenging *our* response to grow more toward His image and likeness. But some of them were addressed to *Him*, inviting *His* response to us. Both can be equally instructive.

In this book we will consider twenty-five questions, and you may find that the answers are not quite what you expect. For example, the question, "Will a man rob God?" is normally used to address the subject of tithes and offerings, but in this discussion it is used in connection with completely different challenges.

The theme scripture of this book commands us to "be of good cheer" (D&C 78:18). My desire is that this collection of question-discussions will not only lead to new ideas and love of the scriptures for the inexhaustible source of inspiration that they are, but more important, to a significant increase in our feelings of happiness, self-acceptance, and fellowship with deity.

—Steven A. Cramer

CHAPTER ONE

WHAT LACK I YET?

> And, behold, one came and said unto him, Good Master, what good thing shall I do, that I may have eternal life?
>
> And he said unto him . . . if thou wilt enter into life, keep the commandments.
>
> He saith unto him, Which? Jesus said, Thou shalt do no murder, thou shalt not commit adultery, Thou shalt not steal, Thou not shalt bear false witness,
>
> Honour thy father and thy mother: and, Thou shalt love they neighbour as thyself.
>
> The young man saith unto him, All these things have I kept from my youth up: what lack I yet? (Matthew 19:16–20)

———————

THIS WAS A man who, though he had kept the commandments from his youth, was honestly seeking further improvement. "What lack I yet?" is a way of asking, what else can I do to please God? How can I make further improvements in my discipleship?

Because "the way of the wicked seduceth them" (Proverbs 12:26), the normal inclination of fallen mankind is to justify and rationalize our sins with an "I'm-doing-okay" and "all-is-well" attitude. Thus Nephi warned, "Wo be unto him that is at ease in Zion! Wo be unto him that crieth: All is well!" (2 Nephi 28:24–25). John referred to this misguided attitude when he spoke of disciples who say, in effect, "I am rich, and increased with goods, and *have need of nothing*" (Revelation 3:17; emphasis added). Because people with this attitude are blind to their own faults, the Lord then warned, "[Thou] knowest not that thou art wretched, and miserable, and poor, and blind, and naked" (Revelation 3:17).

Jesus said it is our knowledge of truth that leads us to freedom (see John 8:32) and that "it is impossible for a man to be saved in ignorance" (D&C 131:6). How could we possibly change or rise above a fault we do not recognize in ourselves? Because "every way of a man [seems] right in his own eyes" (Proverbs 21:2), it takes spiritual maturity to identify our imperfections by sincerely asking, "What lack I yet?"

Another tendency of the natural man is to try to elevate our self-image by looking down on others. We have been commanded to "cease to find fault one with another" (D&C 88:124) and to stop comparing ourselves to others. As Alma counseled, "Do not say: O God, I thank thee that we are better than our brethren; but rather say: O Lord, forgive my unworthiness, and remember my brethren in mercy—yea, *acknowledge your unworthiness before God at all times*" (Alma 38:14; emphasis added). In other words, instead of evaluating ourselves by comparison to others, we should "*examine [ourselves],* whether [we] be in the faith [and] prove [our] own selves" (2 Corinthians 13:5; emphasis added).

"WHAT LACK I YET?"

Whenever we are evaluated by a specialist such as a coach or a doctor, there must always be a diagnosis of our deficiency before a remedy can be applied, but "who can understand his [own] errors?" (Psalm 19:12). No matter how sincerely we try to detect our own lack, we are never able to see ourselves as clearly as Christ sees us, and so we have been challenged to invite His help in identifying the weaknesses we most need to work on next. For example:

- "*Search* me, O God, and know my heart" (Psalm 139:23; emphasis added).
- "*Examine* me, O Lord, and prove me; try my reins" (Proverbs 26:2; emphasis added).
- "O Lord, *correct* me" (Jeremiah 10:24; emphasis added).
- "*Cleanse* thou me from secret faults" (Psalm 19:12; emphasis added).

How wonderful it is to know that the Lord is always there to aid our self-analysis, to help us see what we need in order to grow closer to Him: "And if men come unto me I will show unto them their weakness" (Ether

12:27). This may not seem like a very welcoming response to the effort to draw closer to Him, but it is an act of great kindness. For the Lord said, "My people are destroyed for lack of knowledge" (Hosea 4:6), and "a man is saved no faster than he gets knowledge."[1] "Only in Jesus Christ can any man learn the truth of what he is and how he can be changed from what he is to do the good for which he hopes."[2]

"WHAT LACK I YET?"

We've all experienced the three-sided mirror stations in clothing stores that allow us to view the clothes we are trying on from all sides. We can check the fit and appearance clearer because the three mirrors increase our view. When "the Lord God showeth us our weakness" (Jacob 4:7), it is as if Christ is holding up a three-sided spiritual mirror to help us detect the barriers that have been separating us from Him.

We can see an example of this divine kindness in the Lord's response to William E. McLellan, who inquired of his status before the Lord through the Prophet Joseph Smith. The Lord said, "Verily I say unto you, my servant William, that you are clean, but not all; repent, therefore, of those things which are not pleasing in my sight, saith the Lord, *for the Lord will show them unto you*" (D&C 66:3; emphasis added).

As we open ourselves to this process of divine tutoring, it is wise to remember that there are other kinds of mirrors designed to distort the truth about ourselves. For example, I remember the fun of the carnival mirrors that presented distorted reflections of my appearance as a young boy. One mirror transformed me into an exceedingly tall and skinny person, while the next made me short and round. Such mirrors are fun because we feel safe in the knowledge that the distortions are only pretense. While Christ reveals our true weaknesses as a welcoming invitation to come closer to Him, Satan taunts us with the mental and emotional mirrors of distortion to convince us that we are ugly, inadequate, and inferior.

Another of the devil's favorite weapons could be symbolized by an emotional rearview mirror that holds our attention on the past. When a repentant person is asking, "What lack I yet?" Satan works hard to keep them looking in symbolic rearview mirrors because he knows that a person cannot fix *today* as long as their attention remains focused on *yesterday*.

Although rearview mirrors are helpful for any driver wanting to stay aware of traffic *behind* his moving car, it would be disastrous if most of that driver's attention was focused behind him instead of *forward*, where he wants to go. When Satan gets us to focus too much on the mistakes of our past, that negative focus unwittingly perpetuates the very thing we are trying to overcome because *what holds our attention holds us.* Elder Marvin J. Ashton said, "Where you've been is not nearly as important as where you are and where you're going."[3]

As we discover more about ourselves in the spiritual mirror Christ presents when we come to Him, we face a turning point of decision in the way we respond. Either we turn away from the newly revealed weakness He showed us and retreat back into our comfort zone, or we "turn unto the Lord thy God with all [our] heart, and with all [our] soul" (Deuteronomy 30:10). For example, when Jesus told the sincere man in this chapter's opening scripture, "Yet lackest thou one thing: sell all that thou hast, and distribute unto the poor, and thou shalt have treasure in heaven: and come, follow me," the man "was very sorrowful: for he was very rich" (Luke 18:22–23). How sad that he apparently felt Christ's request was too hard.

We see, then, that as Christ lovingly reveals our weaknesses, "every man may improve upon his talent" (D&C 82:18) and "grow up into him in all things" (Ephesians 4:15), or they can choose to "grow in their iniquities" (Helaman 6:33). But "if we do not improve our time while in this life, then cometh the night of darkness wherein there can be no labor performed" (Alma 34:33).

As we face these choices of growth or retreat, Satan will be ever at our side, taunting us that we are stuck in our faults and cannot change. But that is a lie, because when Christ said, "If men come unto me I will show unto them their weakness," He also said, "I give unto men weakness that they may be humble . . . if they humble themselves before me, and have faith in me, then will I make weak things become strong unto them" (Ether 12:27). As President Benson testified, "There is no human problem beyond His capacity to solve. Because He descended below all things (see D&C 122:8), He knows how to help us rise above our daily difficulties. . . . There is no evil which He cannot arrest."[4]

As the Savior kindly shows us where and how to improve and even offers us the strength to do so, let us, with faith and trust in Him, "come boldly unto the throne of grace, that we may obtain mercy, and find grace to help in time of need" (Hebrews 4:16). Surely, as we pursue this quest with determination, God will never need say to us, "Thou art weighed in the balances, and art found wanting" (Daniel 5:27).

"WHAT LACK I YET?"

Conclusion: How could applying the principles taught by this chapter's question help you to feel better about yourself, improve your relationship with the Lord, and lead you to greater feelings of happiness and peace?

NOTES

1. Joseph Smith, *Teachings of the Prophet Joseph Smith*, sel. by Joseph Fielding Smith (Salt Lake City: Deseret Book, 1951), 217.
2. *In His Footsteps Today*, Gospel Doctrine manual (Salt Lake City: Deseret Sunday School Union, 1969), 4.
3. As quoted in Sheri L. Dew, "As Elder Statesman," *This People Magazine*, March/April 1984, 27.
4. "Jesus Christ: Our Savior and Redeemer," *Ensign*, November 1983, 8.

CHAPTER TWO

WILT THOU BE MADE WHOLE?

Now there is at Jerusalem by the sheep market a pool, which is called in the Hebrew tongue Bethesda, having five porches.

In these lay a great multitude of impotent folk, of blind, halt, withered, waiting for the moving of the water.

For an angel went down at a certain season into the pool, and troubled the water: whosoever then first after the troubling of the water stepped in was made whole of whatsoever disease he had.

And a certain man was there, which had an infirmity thirty and eight years.

When Jesus saw him lie, and knew he had been now a long time in that case, he saith unto him, Wilt thou be made whole?

The impotent man answered him, Sir, I have no man, when the water is troubled, to put me into the pool: but while I am coming, another steppeth down before me.

Jesus saith unto him, Rise, take up thy bed, and walk.

And immediately the man was made whole, and took up his bed, and walked. (John 5:2–9)

———————

"WILT THOU BE made whole?" This question changed my life dramatically because it taught me to stop praying about *symptoms* and start seeking the higher quest of fully coming to His image. Bethesda was a mineral pool in Jerusalem where many people waited, hoping for physical healing. The people who went there for healing believed that "an angel went down at a certain season into the pool, and troubled the water," and that whichever person was first into the agitated water "was made whole of whatsoever disease he had" (John 5:4). Whether these healings occurred because of the periodic agitation of the mineral waters or because of the faith of the people (or a combination of both), it would appear that enough people were healed that many were willing to spend months and even years on those porches, waiting for the chance of being the first one into the water.

This large group of hopeful believers included the man who was about to receive Christ's question about becoming whole. How many times during this poor man's thirty-eight years of affliction had he lain there on those ledges, or porches, hoping for a turn in the healing waters? But because of his particular paralysis or crippled condition, he was always too slow to be the first to reach the water. Through all those long years, each time the waters were agitated, he had attempted to crawl from his ledge, but because he had no one to help him, the other, more able-bodied hopefuls had crowded him away in their understandable quest to be first. For thirty-eight years he had waited and hoped but never received the healing. How many of us could sustain an unanswered faith that long? He certainly had great perseverance, but this was probably a man who felt very discouraged, a man whose feelings of despair could represent our own burdens of distress.

When Jesus saw him lying there "and knew that he had been now a long time in that case, he saith unto him, Wilt thou be made whole?" (John 5:6). Perhaps the people laughed or mocked the Savior for asking such an obvious question. Of course the man wanted to be healed. "The impotent man answered him, Sir, I have no man, when the water is troubled, to put me into the pool: but while I am coming, another steppeth down before me" (John 5:7).

But perhaps the Savior's question was not about being healed of his *crippled* condition so that he could walk. That was obvious. Could it be that the real question for this man was whether he was willing to go inside himself and be healed of his *spiritual burdens*, his accumulation of heartaches and grudges? It was whether he was willing to let go of all the bitterness and angry questions about why God had allowed this infirmity in the first place, as well as those thirty-eight years of wasted, lonely pleadings. What good would it have done the man if his legs were healed but not his heart? "Wilt thou be made whole?" What a kind question this was. It is a question that challenges every disciple of Christ.

Perhaps for us who are so skilled at praying about outward symptoms, the implication of this question is that there are some disciples who are *not* willing to be whole. Why? Why would anyone want to be incomplete? Why would any disciple of Christ choose to go partway toward the Savior but hold back and not go all the way to wholeness and the fulness of joy and perfection He is offering? It is because some of us prefer to remain in the comfortable pain of our present circumstances rather than face the unknown challenges of growth and change.

C. S. Lewis said, "It may be hard for an egg to turn into a bird: it would be a jolly sight harder for it to learn to fly while remaining an egg. We are like eggs at present. And you cannot go on indefinitely being just an ordinary, decent egg. We must be hatched or go bad."[1] It is this lifelong process of being hatched, or transformed from the fallen, natural-man state into the image and likeness of Christ that confronts each of us with the daily choice of becoming whole—or only going partway.

How often we come to God seeking only the release of our pain, praying about *symptoms* rather than about becoming whole—seeking *relief* instead of expansion and growth. For example, you might say, "Please help me stop smoking, drinking, doing drugs, or viewing pornography. Please help me to stop cussing. Help me with my temper. Help me to stop yelling at my kids." Certainly these are righteous desires and represent the surface kinds of imperfections that we should be striving to overcome. But they are only *symptoms*—symptoms of the hollowness and spiritual bankruptcy inside every fallen, natural man and woman who needs to be born again into the wholeness of Christ's image and likeness.

There is an incredible spiritual difference between praying to stop committing a particular *sin* and praying and working to rise above our *sinfulness* and *sinful nature*. When we only pray about symptoms, it is like we are trying to remain eggs. Better eggs, yes, but not transformed eggs. How many addicts, for example, have tried to escape drugs, alcohol, or pornography, praying desperately to abandon the harmful behavior but never breaking free because all their emotions and thoughts are focused on the outward symptoms rather than the more important inward need for the divine change of heart and nature that makes us whole? Looking back, I can see that one of the reasons I could not overcome my addictions for over thirty years, in spite of great effort and determination, was this mistaken focus on symptoms instead of *wholeness*.[2]

I found that there is a life-transforming and liberating difference between being willing to let go of a particular sin (merely an outward change of behavior) and surrendering all the accompanying burdens to the

Savior's Atonement. My conclusion from working with people in addiction and spiritual agony is that true healing can only occur when there is total surrender of *all* the burdens that are creating barriers between the Lord and us—burdens like self-pity, guilt, worthlessness, and inferiority, every burden of self-punishment that keeps us from becoming whole.

God desires perfect joy and fulfillment for each one of us. That is why His way always involves changing us *inside* more than simply changing our *outward* checklist of behaviors. What changed my life was discovering that the Savior is not offering us *relief*, but *conquest* and *transformation*. And that no matter how sincerely we pray for release from our pain, He will settle for nothing less than the removal of its cause. The reason "the Lord requireth the [totally committed] heart and a willing mind" is that we cannot develop the spirituality that will prepare us for celestial life with a halfhearted effort any more than we could sustain physical life with a heart that only beat part-time instead of twenty-four hours a day (D&C 64:34). That is why the Lord is asking for disciples "who know their hearts are honest, and are broken, and their spirits contrite, and are willing to observe their covenants by sacrifice—yea, every sacrifice which I, the Lord, shall command" (D&C 97:8).

This total submission to the Lord's will for us means we are so determined to become *whole* that we are willing to bear our tutoring and refining "crosses" no matter how great the sacrifice, no matter how heavy the load, and no matter how hard or long the labor required to change us into His image and wholeness. It means we not only have a willingness, but also a desire to place our hearts and our wills, our entire selves, upon the altar of sacrifice without knowing, or even caring, what the Lord will require of us. The transforming "I-don't-care-what-sacrifice-is-required-of-me-as-long-as-God-is-directing-it" attitude of total submission is exemplified by the words of the prophet Ether, who said, "Whether the Lord will that I be translated, or that I suffer the will of the Lord in the flesh, it mattereth not, if it so be that I am saved in the kingdom of God" (Ether 15:34). It is also illustrated by Lamoni's father, a cruel and wicked king who, when touched by the Lord's Spirit, made the totally yielding and trusting commitment: "I will give away all my sins to know thee" (Alma 22:18).

Being rescued from my own addictions and more than twenty years of helping others conquer theirs through the power of Christ has taught me that, ultimately, *being made whole* means being molded and perfected into the Savior's image and character, for only when we are completely like Him will we be completely whole. That's why the Lord is constantly working to help us achieve personal victory over anything and everything that prevents us from being like Him and having the perfect wholeness of joy and peace that He enjoys.

"WILT THOU BE MADE WHOLE?"

Conclusion: How could applying the principles taught by this chapter's question help you to feel better about yourself, improve your relationship with the Lord, and lead you to greater feelings of happiness and peace?

NOTES

1. C. S. Lewis, *Mere Christianity*, 29th ed. (New York: MacMillan Publishing Company, 1979), 169–70.
2. For a personal account of the author's recovery, see Steven A. Cramer, *The Worth of a Soul*.

CHAPTER THREE

WHERE ART THOU?

And when the woman saw that the tree was good for food, and that it was pleasant to the eyes, and a tree to be desired to make one wise, she took of the fruit thereof, and did eat, and gave also unto her husband with her; and he did eat.

And the eyes of them both were opened, and they knew that they were naked; and they sewed fig leaves together, and made themselves aprons.

And they heard the voice of the Lord God walking in the garden in the cool of the day: and Adam and his wife hid themselves from the presence of the Lord God amongst the trees of the garden.

And the Lord God called unto Adam, and said unto him, Where art thou?

And he said, I heard thy voice in the garden, and I was afraid, because I was naked; and I hid myself. (Genesis 3:6–10)

ONE OF TWO things happens to every person who disobeys God. Either they are drawn back to Him with humble and contrite remorse, intent on repentance with hearts that are broken for being less than God expected of them, less than they intended to be, or they follow the natural-man trait to slink away in unresolved guilt, looking for ways to hide from God.

Adam and Eve had been given permission to eat of the fruit of all the trees in the garden but one, the tree that would introduce blood into their bodies, slowly transforming them into mortals. They would lose innocence, become subject to sin, and gain knowledge of good and evil. As Elder James E. Talmage explained, "The man

13

and the woman had now become mortal; through indulgence in food unsuited to their nature and condition and against which they had been specifically warned, and as the inevitable result of their disobeying the divine law and commandment, they became liable to the physical ailments and bodily frailties to which mankind has since been the natural heir."[1]

When they disobeyed the commandment and partook of the forbidden fruit, they quickly gained knowledge of two things. First was the discovery that they were naked. The second and far more important discovery was the knowledge of what it is like to feel unworthy and ashamed before the Lord.

How perfectly Adam and Eve's response typifies the natural man's self-defeating attempts at escape. When they heard Heavenly Father's voice as He approached, they grabbed some large fig leaves to cover their nakedness, and then "Adam and his wife hid themselves from the presence of the Lord God amongst the trees of the garden" (Genesis 3:8). This verse would be more accurate if it said they *tried* to hide themselves, which is an act of futility, for nothing can be hidden from God. Not only does He see our actions, but He is also aware of the very thoughts and intents of our hearts (see Proverbs 15:3; Jeremiah 16:17; 23:24; D&C 88:109).

One purpose of this probationary life is to learn the lessons of mortality as a kind Father holds us accountable for our choices. And so He called, "Adam, where art thou?" The Lord knew very well where Adam and Eve were hiding, quivering in fear, but He wanted them to grow through the process of confession and self-discovery, just as He pleads for us to do today.

Adam gave the same reason for hiding from God that prompts us to try and hide when we do things we know are wrong and unworthy of true disciples: "I was afraid, because I was naked; and I hid myself" (Genesis 3:10). Which is the same as saying, "I was afraid and ashamed because I knew I had been disobedient and I didn't want to face you. Because I feared you more than trusted you, I hid." Eventually Adam would learn, as must we all, that the issue is not that we make mistakes—for that is part of the divine design of this mortal school. The issue is whether we allow the guilt we then feel to *push us away* from God, as Adam and Eve did, or whether it *draws us to Him* with the broken heart that makes forgiveness and progress possible. Paul explained the difference between true remorse and fig-leaf remorse:

> Now I rejoice, not that ye were made sorry, but that ye sorrowed to repentance: for ye were made sorry after a godly manner. . . .
>
> For godly sorrow worketh repentance to salvation not to be repented of: but the sorrow of the world worketh death. (2 Corinthians 7:9–10)

The fact that evil tempts us does not prove that we are unworthy. It only verifies that we are mortal. Sin appeals to every "natural" man and woman, and from time to time everyone, including the most devout, makes choices that are unworthy of a disciple. Because learning from our mistakes is such an important part of this mortal experience, scripture says, "Blessed are they who will repent and turn unto me" (Helaman 13:11), and "Blessed is he whose transgression is forgiven, whose sin is covered" (Psalm 32:1; also Romans 4:7). Nowhere do the scriptures say, or even hint, "Blessed is he who never needs to repent or receive forgiveness," for only Christ was in that position.

Adam and Eve tried to hide their nakedness with aprons of fig leaves. Too often we devise our own fig-leaf aprons to hide our mistakes, bad habits, and favorite sins. Usually we call them false fronts instead of fig-leaf aprons. A false front could range from something as innocent as wearing a smile and acting as if things are okay when they are not, to the hypocrisy of pretending to be righteous instead of repenting and really living an honest life of spirituality. Thus, many "aprons" of hypocrisy may be sewn of good works that appear to be noble and righteous but which are as empty as "sounding brass" because they were not done with real intent or sincere love and devotion to Christ and His cause (see 1 Corinthians 13).

The Savior is always concerned about *what* we do, but He is even more concerned about *why* we do it. Pretending to be what we are not or trying to hide from the Lord behind a false front will never improve one's life. Because the purpose of all we do in the Church should be to help ourselves and others to become more like Christ, Alma taught that when men are judged and rewarded "according to their works," they will be judged not merely by what they have *done*, but also according to what they *are*. "For the time is at hand," he said, "that all men shall reap a reward of their works, according to that which they have *been*" (Alma 9:28; emphasis added).

"WHERE ART THOU?"

The Pearl of Great Price account of this event does not use that question. It states that it was not after Adam and Eve had hidden that God asked where they were, but it was at the very moment that "Adam and his wife went to hide themselves from the presence of the Lord God amongst the trees of the garden" (Moses 4:14) that the Lord lovingly interrupted their attempt at escape, asking not "Where art thou?" but "Where goest thou?" (Moses 4:15).

Today the Lord's questions of "Where art thou?" or "Where are you going?" come to us more often through our conscience than they do audibly. Just as modern cars are equipped with warning lights to alert us to malfunctions and pending damage to our cars, the Lord has equipped our minds with the "warning light" of conscience: "Now, there was a punishment affixed, and a just law given, which brought remorse of conscience unto man" (Alma 42:18).

"Where art thou?" and "Where goest thou?" are important questions because of the natural man's tendency to hide behind our own puny, futile fig-leaf aprons as literally as Adam and Eve did. And unless we change our choices, we will end up exactly where we are headed. Are our present choices and priorities pointing us upward toward the celestial kingdom or downward toward the terrestrial or telestial? The gift of godly sorrow, which comes through the conscience, is sent to alert us to the dangers of improper thought patterns and choices that could result in spiritual damage to our eternal souls. But unlike the blinking light in our car's dash, the conscience is not only able to warn us, but also to help us feel uncomfortable with our sin and move us to repentance (see 2 Corinthians 7:9–10).

Satan and his demons, however, have become very skilled at misdirecting the warning light of conscience. His demons are forever hovering about us, eagerly waiting to ridicule every mistake; eager to whisper lies about our weaknesses and improper choices that prompt us to hide instead of confessing and changing. They would have us believe that it is safer and more comfortable to hide in the darkness of isolation, substituting the apron of self-condemnation for the majesty of Christ's Atonement and forgiveness that comes with confession and repentance. How pleased they are when we hide behind that apron, saying to God, "Do you see how angry I am with myself over my weaknesses and sins? Do you see how miserable I am making myself to please you?" What a horrible distortion that is.

True guilt, the righteous godly sorrow that God sends through the conscience, is healthy and will always pull us back toward repentance and a strengthened relationship with Christ and Heavenly Father. If we really believe in the Lord's love, we will ignore Satan's lies and come running to the Lord with our mistakes, asking Him for help instead of trying to hide. But if we accept Satan's lies, we soon forget about God's love; we forget about His mercy and plan of repentance and forgiveness. We will have false guilt: the distorted, over-emphasized, self-condemning fig-leaf guilt that causes us to hide from God that comes from Satan.

It is no use pretending that we can hide behind our false aprons of disguise. Like it or not, God knows what is going on in our lives better than we do. Like the three-sided mirrors provided in clothing stores so that we can twist and turn to view ourselves from all sides and test how we look, the weekly sacrament service is a wonderful time to do the same thing, taking a look inside as we ask ourselves where we are and where are we going. How did I do in keeping my covenants this week? What could I have done better? What improvements should I work on during the coming week? "Where art thou?"

The only way to remedy the problems we discover in that self-examination is to break ourselves—to break our very hearts—by coming to Him just as we are, fully acknowledging our weaknesses, faults, sins, bad habits, indeed our entire unworthiness and need for Him to help us change. We must "acknowledge [our] unworthiness before God at all times" (Alma 38:14). The amazing and joyful truth is that when we do come out from behind our aprons to come to Him honestly and openly, He responds much faster than when we attempt to hold our faults behind our backs, as if He didn't know about them.

"WHERE ART THOU?"

Conclusion: How could applying the principles taught by this chapter's question help you to feel better about yourself, improve your relationship with the Lord, and lead you to greater feelings of happiness and peace?

NOTES

1. James E. Talmage, *Jesus the Christ*, 25th ed. (Salt Lake City: Deseret Book, 1956), 19.

CHAPTER FOUR

WHERE ARE THOSE THINE ACCUSERS?

And early in the morning he came again into the temple, and all the people came unto him; and he sat down, and taught them.

And the scribes and Pharisees brought unto him a woman taken in adultery; and when they had set her in the midst, They say unto him, Master, this woman was taken in adultery, in the very act.

Now Moses in the law commanded us, that such should be stoned: but what sayest thou?

This they said, tempting him, that they might have to accuse him. But Jesus stooped down, and with his finger wrote on the ground, as though he heard them not.

So when they continued asking him, he lifted up himself, and said unto them, He that is without sin among you, let him first cast a stone at her.

And again he stooped down, and wrote on the ground.

And they which heard it, being convicted by their own conscience, went out one by one, beginning at the eldest, even unto the last: and Jesus was left alone, and the woman standing in the midst.

When Jesus had lifted up himself, and saw none but the woman, he said unto her, Woman, where are those thine accusers? hath no man condemned thee?

She said, No man, Lord. And Jesus said unto her, Neither do I condemn thee: go, and sin no more. (John 8:2–11)

———————

THE SAVIOR ASKED the question, "Where are those thine accusers?" of one who could represent many of us, a woman who was most likely hanging her head in embarrassment as she wept in shame for having her sin exposed not only in public, but in the temple itself. This question changed my life, because for over thirty years I lived with that kind of unresolved guilt and fear.

. This question was occasioned by one of many attempts to trap the Savior. Throughout His three-year ministry, the jealous scribes and Pharisees were continually "laying wait for him, and seeking to catch something out of his mouth" that would enable them to "find an accusation against him" (Luke 11:54; 6:7). Having been unsuccessful so many times in challenging His interpretations of the law, they must have felt very confident confronting Him with a woman who was taken in the very act of adultery, a sin that ranks in seriousness only after murder and denying the Holy Ghost (see Alma 39:5; how interesting that they did not bring the guilty man to the temple for judgment as well).

This was one of their more clever traps because it appeared that no matter what answer or judgment Jesus might give, He was trapped between agreeing with the penalty of death by stoning that was prescribed in the law of Moses or agreeing with the restrictions of the Roman law, which then prevented such penalties. If He said she must be stoned per the ancient law, they could accuse Him of defying Roman authority. On the other hand, if He showed her the mercy and opportunity to repent that He was so well known for, they could accuse Him of not respecting the law of Moses. Hence, it appeared that He was trapped.

If Christ were not a God of love, mercy, and forgiveness, we might have expected Him to join in the accusing condemnation. "So, you've filthied yourself with the greatest sin there is next to murder! How in the world did you ever fall to this level? Are you sorry? Have you learned your lesson?" This kind of fear and false expectation was one of the major factors that kept me from understanding what a kind and loving God our Savior is. But those were not His words. I have learned that those will never be His words because Christ is concerned less with the mistakes we make than He is with having things made right with Him. I am grateful to finally understand that He is more interested in what we have learned and how we want to live from now on. Therefore, instead of confronting the woman or shaming her in the presence of others, He avoided the trap by laying the burden of judgment upon their own consciences. To her self-righteous accusers He challenged protectively, "He that is without sin among you, let him first cast a stone at her." Convicted by their own consciences, they each turned in shame and "went out one by one" (John 8:7, 9; emphasis added).

When Jesus and the woman were left alone, He asked with tender compassion, "Woman, where are those thine accusers?" And now we can see that the relevance of this question was its introduction of the next one: "Hath no man condemned thee?" The importance of those two questions is their combined introduction to the stunning statement that followed. When she reported that none of those self-righteous and angry men could overlook their own sins to condemn hers, Christ showed that His concern was not for the woman's sin so much as for rescuing her soul. "Jesus said unto her, *Neither do I condemn thee*: go, and sin no more" (John 8:11; emphasis added).

That divine statement is contrary to what the natural man would expect Him to say. It is not difficult to expect God's mercy and forgiveness when we confess and repent of normal human weaknesses and unintentional sins. Yet one of the most unfortunate and unnecessary barriers to our spiritual progression is our mistaken expectation of divine condemnation for our deliberate sins. It is true that the Lord has commanded us to seek perfection in our daily discipleship, but He is not demanding the attainment of that perfection before He will love or bless us. Consider the harsh dictionary definitions of *accuse* and *condemn*: To charge with a shortcoming, an error, or wrongdoing. To express strong disapproval, to find guilty, to pronounce judgment and sentence against, to declare to be unfit. To incriminate, blame, criticize, complain against, reproach, reprove, censure, indict, denounce, and condemn.

There is nothing divine or loving in those painful words. Christ has often demonstrated that His purpose is never to put us down or condemn us for our weaknesses or sins, but to save us from them, to strengthen and encourage us, to heal us of our infirmities and sorrows, to lift us toward His level of perfection and joy. He said, for example, "The Son of man is come to seek and to save that which was lost," and "joy shall be in heaven over one sinner that repenteth, more than over ninety and nine just persons, which need no repentance" (Luke 19:10; 15:7). Yes, He has such strict standards that He "cannot look upon sin with the least degree of allowance" (D&C 1:31). But the wonderful assurance of the scriptures is that He has infinite allowance, He has infinite tolerance, compassion and mercy, infinite patience and forgiveness for every repentant person.

There is never a trace of condemnation in His perfect and unwavering love. One of the discoveries that changed my life was learning that God doesn't demand that we overcome every fault before He loves us, because He knows that if we need changing, discovering His love for us will lead us to change.

When I finally let go of my false beliefs, I found that the non-condemning arms of His loving acceptance are always open and inviting us to come to Him. Lehi testified, "Because thou art merciful, thou wilt not suffer those who come unto thee that they shall perish!" (1 Nephi 1:14). Christ affirmed that testimony when He promised, "Him that cometh to me I will in no wise cast out" (John 6:37). But what if we come stained with unconquered sins like the woman taken in adultery? Then He helps us to conquer and rise above them. That's who He is. That is what He does. "Thou art not excusable in thy transgressions," He said, "nevertheless, go thy way and sin no more" (D&C 24:2).

For example, the apostle John witnessed in his testimony that "God sent not his Son into the world to *condemn* the world; but that the world through him might be *saved*" (John 3:17; emphasis added). And the Savior Himself assured us: "Behold, *I do not condemn you*; go your ways and sin no more; perform with soberness the work which I have commanded you" (D&C 6:35; emphasis added).

When we make mistakes, Satan tries to make us feel like worthless junk. Our family has been involved twice in automobile accidents with damage so severe that the insurance adjusters almost considered our car "totaled" because the cost of the repairs was so close to the value of the car that it would have been easier to just scrap it rather than repair it. For over thirty years I felt like worthless junk, but Jesus never "totals" or "scraps" anyone to the junk pile. No mistake or bad choice can diminish our value in His sight or put us beyond His power to repair and make us new. *Better than new.*

Are you one who has been lost? Have bad choices and spiritual defeats caused you to condemn yourself or feel that God has condemned you? How can you know if your feelings of guilt are healthy or harmful? How can you be sure if they are appropriate or inappropriate? The way to tell is incredibly simple. True guilt moves us to repentance and pulls us *back* to God, while false guilt, the distorted, over-emphasized, self-condemning guilt, pulls us down and builds barriers between us and God. Christ left His throne of glory to suffer and die for us. Our value to the Savior is priceless, so what right do we have to judge ourselves as unworthy? "For the Lord your God is gracious and merciful, and will not turn away his face from you, if ye return unto him" (2 Chronicles 30:9).

Are you struggling with a need you cannot fill, a weakness or sin you have not been able to conquer, a hurt or emotional wound that is festering because you cannot heal it yourself? Then you are the one Christ is looking for. Will you come to the Shepherd? Will you accept His invitation? Will you bring all your emptiness and heartache to Him and exchange it for the joy of knowing His love and forgiveness? He is waiting with open arms to receive you in the same manner He received this woman.

"WHERE ARE THOSE THINE ACCUSERS?"

Conclusion: How could applying the principles taught by this chapter's question help you to feel better about yourself, improve your relationship with the Lord, and lead you to greater feelings of happiness and peace?

CHAPTER FIVE

BETRAYEST THOU THE SON OF MAN WITH A KISS?

Rise, let us be going: behold, he is at hand that doth betray me.

And while he yet spake, lo, Judas, one of the twelve, came, and with him a great multitude with swords and staves, from the chief priests and elders of the people.

Now he that betrayed him gave them a sign, saying, Whomsoever I shall kiss, that same is he: hold him fast.

And forthwith he came to Jesus, and said, Hail, master; and kissed him. (Matthew 26:46–49)

But Jesus said unto him, Judas, betrayest thou the Son of man with a kiss? (Luke 22:48)

ADVERTISING AGENCIES SPECIALIZE in creating brand imprints. For example, say the word *Xerox*, and people know instantly that you're referring to a copy machine. Calling someone a Judas attaches the unmistakable imprint of traitor. Just as there are many brands of copy machines, there are also many brands of traitors. While it is unlikely that a person reading a book such as this would intentionally betray the Savior as Judas did, we want to consider a couple of ways that show how easy it is to betray Him unintentionally.

Having left the last supper to coordinate the arrest with the conspirators, Judas led them to the Garden of Gethsemane, where Jesus had initiated the Atonement, suffering the anguish and pain of our sins. In the dark of night came the traitor, "one of the twelve, and with him a great multitude with swords and staves, from the chief priests and the scribes and the elders" (Mark 14:43). Knowing there would be uncertainty in identifying Christ among His apostles, Judas gave the mob a way to be certain they arrested the right man: "Whomsoever I shall kiss, that same is he; take him, and lead him away safely" (Mark 14:44).

One of the most tender, intimate things we can do with our lips is to kiss someone. A kiss can express friendship, family love, passionate feelings, even respect, as with those who have had the privilege of kissing Christ's feet (see Luke 7:38; 3 Nephi 11:19; 17:10). In that ancient culture, such a kiss was considered a greeting of the highest regard and respect. To give or to accept such a kiss was an expression of integrity and trust between the two parties (for examples, see Exodus 4:27; Luke 7:45; Romans 16:16).

That hypocritical betrayal-kiss by Judas is, undoubtedly, the most famous kiss in all of history. More than the act of betrayal by one of the inner circle of disciples, it was the insult of the kiss that has put the stamp of treachery on his name even more than the deed.

The scriptures often use the lips to symbolize pretense and hypocrisy. Speaking of the false creeds taught by apostate churches and ministers, the Lord told Joseph Smith, "They draw near to me with their lips, but their hearts are far from me" (JS—H 1:19; emphasis added; see also Isaiah 29:13; Matthew 15:8; 2 Nephi 27:25). Truly Judas "drew near" to the Lord with his lips, but his heart and loyalty were far from Him as he said, "Hail, master; and kissed him" (Matthew 26:49). And then "Jesus said unto him, Judas, betrayest thou the Son of man with a kiss?" (Luke 22:48).

Some have thought this betrayal was simply the result of his own dissatisfaction or confusion, but John testified that it was "the devil [who] put into the heart of Judas Iscariot, Simon's son, to betray him" (John 13:2). Satan's power to influence our thoughts and values is a danger we all face (see 2 Nephi 28:20–23). He and his demons are continually trying to put suggestions into our hearts to betray our spouses, families, Church, and God, by breaking our covenants and choosing the ways of the world over trustworthy obedience, loyal service, and sacrifice. Joseph Fielding Smith warned, "We should be on guard always to resist Satan's advances. . . . He has power to place thoughts in our minds and to whisper to us in unspoken impressions to entice us to satisfy our appetites or desires and in various other ways he plays upon our weaknesses and desires."[1]

We've all heard the saying, "His word is his bond." Unfortunately, that ethic belongs more to a previous culture than it does to ours. It is easy to condemn Judas for the traitorous way he used his lips, but betraying lips have become an epidemic in our society. Many husbands and wives, for example, betray their sacred marriage vows by sharing kisses and other intimacies with companions besides the one to whom they were promised.

"BETRAYEST THOU THE SON OF MAN WITH A KISS?"

Mormon grieved over those whose hearts become so hardened that they "do forget the Lord their God, and do trample under their feet the Holy One" (Helaman 12:2). The treachery of betrayal by Judas comes to mind, but Nephi asked us to examine the more personal implications of betrayal through mere indifference or lack of devotion to the Savior when He said, "Yea, even the very God of Israel do men trample under their feet; I say, trample under their feet but I would speak in other words— *they set him at naught, and hearken not to the voice of his counsels*" (1 Nephi 19:7; emphasis added). Thus a common form of betrayal lies in lukewarm indifference and breaking our promises to Him.

One of the attributes of God's perfection is His absolute commitment to deliver on every word He speaks and to keep every promise He makes, regardless of opposing circumstances, for "it is impossible for him to deny his word" (Alma 11:34), "he executeth all his words" (2 Nephi 9:17), and "the Lord God will fulfil his covenants which he has made unto his children" (2 Nephi 6:12). Surely the Lord has a right to expect the same of us. If we promise something to the Lord, He should be able to count on us to do it. Following His example, we should be willing to say, "I have opened my mouth unto the Lord, *and I cannot go back*" (Judges 11:35; emphasis added).

Scriptures emphasize, "When thou vowest a vow unto God, defer not to pay it . . . [for] *better is it that thou shouldest not vow, than that thou shouldest vow and not pay*" (Ecclesiastes 5:4–5; emphasis added). Why would it be better not to make a covenant than to make it and then deliberately break it? Because that would be an act of hypocrisy and betrayal for which we would be held accountable, "For I, the Lord, am not to be mocked in the last days" (D&C 63:58). Mocking someone is defined as treating him or her with ridicule or contempt, or disappointing someone by letting down his or her hopes.

The betrayal by Judas was public and immediately recognized. Our betrayals are usually more private. While they may not always be recognized by our peers, they are always known to the Lord. "Behold," He warned, "there are hypocrites among you, who have deceived some . . . but *the hypocrites shall be detected* and shall be cut off, either in life or in death, even as I will" (D&C 50:7–8; emphasis added). Many of the Second Coming destructions will be specifically targeted at Church members who have betrayed the Lord and the Church with hypocritical false fronts.

> Behold, vengeance cometh speedily upon the inhabitants of the earth, a day of wrath, a day of burning, a day of desolation, of weeping, of mourning, and of lamentation; and as a whirlwind it shall come upon all the face of the earth, saith the Lord.
>
> *And upon my house shall it begin*, and from my house shall it go forth, saith the Lord;
>
> *First among those among you, saith the Lord, who have professed to know my name and have not known me*, and have blasphemed against me in the midst of my house, saith the Lord. (D&C 112:24–26; emphasis added)

A person can spend years, even a lifetime, learning to trust God, but how much effort do we invest in making ourselves trustworthy to him? "Arise up and *be more careful henceforth in observing your vows*, which you have made and do make," the Lord challenged, "and you shall be blessed with exceeding great blessings" (D&C 108:3; emphasis added). But "when thou shalt vow a vow unto the Lord thy God, thou shalt not slack to pay it: *for the Lord thy God will surely require it of thee; and it would be sin in thee*" (Deuteronomy 23:21; emphasis added).

"BETRAYEST THOU THE SON OF MAN WITH A KISS?"

Conclusion: How could applying the principles taught by this chapter's question help you to feel better about yourself, improve your relationship with the Lord, and lead you to greater feelings of happiness and peace?

NOTES

1. Joseph Fielding Smith, *Answers to Gospel Questions* (Salt Lake City: Deseret Book, 1957–66), 3:81.

CHAPTER SIX

WHO TOUCHED ME?

And a woman having an issue of blood twelve years, which had spent all her living upon physicians, neither could be healed of any,

Came behind him, and touched the border of his garment: and immediately her issue of blood stanched.

And Jesus said, Who touched me? When all denied, Peter and they that were with him said, Master, the multitude throng thee and press thee, and sayest thou, Who touched me?

And Jesus said, Somebody hath touched me: for I perceive that virtue is gone out of me.

And when the woman saw that she was not hid, she came trembling, and falling down before him, she declared unto him before all the people for what cause she had touched him, and how she was healed immediately.

And he said unto her, Daughter, be of good comfort: thy faith hath made thee whole; go in peace. (Luke 8:43–48; also Matthew 9:18–22; Mark 5:21–34)

ON THE NORTHWESTERN shore of the Sea of Galilee was a large city called Capernaum. One day, while Jesus was teaching a large gathering along the shore of the sea, a visitor of great importance interrupted the group. It was Jairus, one of the rulers of the Jewish synagogue there in Capernaum. Jairus had come to ask the Savior to come to his home and heal his only daughter, a child of twelve years, who lay in bed only moments from death.

This was truly remarkable, because it was so often the rulers of the synagogues who led the ridicule and opposition to the Savior's mission.

Jairus had been unable to find a physician who could heal the girl, and even though he knew he should be regarded as one "in the camp of the enemy," he now risked his reputation, casting aside all pride and status, and threw himself at Christ's feet, worshiping Him and begging Him to heal his daughter. This was an extraordinary missionary opportunity. Jesus agreed to interrupt His teaching, and they left immediately on this urgent rescue mission.

Eager to witness the miracle, the crowd followed them. In fact, there were so many people in the crowd, each one trying to be close to the Lord, that it must have been difficult for Him to walk (see Mark 5:24).

In this crowd was a woman who also needed a divine rescue—a woman we could say represents each of us. She must have wanted to be near the Savior, to look into His face and to feel of His love, just as we would. But this she could not do because, according to Jewish law, she was unclean. For twelve years she had suffered a vaginal flow of blood, an almost constant hemorrhage. The woman's sickness was a terrible burden, but perhaps even worse than the physical weakness and suffering caused by this plague was the mental and emotional shame inflicted by the public scorn it had brought upon her. Judged unfit for marriage, unfit to mingle with the community, unfit to worship in the temple, she was regarded as an outcast, worthless and unclean, for in the Mosaic law, a woman was treated as unclean during her normal monthly cycle. And if for any reason there were to be a continued flow of blood beyond that normal cycle, she would continue to be considered unclean and unfit to be touched for as long as that lasted, much less to be considered for marriage (see Leviticus 15:19–27).

According to Mark's account, during those twelve long years of illness, she had spent all her money going from one physician to another, always hoping that the next one would have a cure. But none of them had an answer. The scriptures say that she suffered many things at the hands of the doctors, things that were sometimes worse, perhaps, than the illness itself. For all her money and humiliation, her plague had only grown worse (see Mark 5:25–34). Now, after twelve long and lonely years, there was only one hope left, and that was Jesus. But unlike the blind or the crippled, which called so boldly for His help, she dared not ask. She was not even supposed to be out in public. Jewish law had labeled her unclean. She must have felt separated from Jesus by a crowd of clean people.

Many people have felt that way; that they aren't good enough to be with the Lord; that because of their mistakes they are unworthy to ask for His help; that surely He would want only the clean, moral, righteous people around Him; that they are forever separated by what the others *are* and they are *not*. There is good news for people with such feelings, because that is exactly the kind of people the Lord specializes in. He frequently said the reason He came was to seek and to save those who were lost, those who most needed His help (see Matthew 9:13; Luke 15:7; 19:10).

So great was this woman's faith in Christ's divine power that "she said within herself, If I may but touch his garment, I shall be whole" (Matthew 9:21). She was free to receive His loving help because she had no more defenses, no more substitutes, no more hope but Him. It is to that same point of broken heart and contrite spirit that we also must come, and when we do we will be ready for the message of this woman's experience.

You know the story. She did manage to push her way through the crowd, probably covering her face so as not to be recognized. And when she touched His robe she felt the flow of blood stop. Immediately she knew she was healed. But then, to her horror, Jesus, who was rushing to heal the dying daughter of Jairus, suddenly stopped and asked one of the most interesting questions in all of scripture: "Who touched me?"

Incredulous, his disciples asked, "Thou seest the multitude thronging thee, and sayest thou, Who touched me?" (Mark 5:31). As His eyes searched the crowd for her, He explained that this touch was different; that it was a touch of faith; that He had actually felt virtue or power flow from His body.

"Who touched me?" There are other ways to ask that question. Who trusted in My power? Who believed in Me? Who applied their faith and made claim upon the blessings I am so anxious to share with each of my brothers and sisters? "Who touched me?"

This simple question teaches us volumes about the Lord, about who He is and what He is like. It shows, for example, that *nothing* escapes His notice. It demonstrates that no act of faith goes unnoticed, that no matter where He is, no matter what He is doing, He will *never* miss the petition of one in need. This question tells us that He can be pressed in a crowd, He can be occupied with important matters, like saving the life of a dying child and influencing the stubborn and blind Jewish leaders—and yet know in an instant when He has been touched by one in need. It shows that it is the poor and needy, the hurting and hopeless, that come first in His priorities (see Luke 4:18). And perhaps most important, it demonstrates that it is okay to interrupt God. Our prayers do not bother Him when we plead for help.

***

"WHO TOUCHED ME?"

***

The movement stopped. The crowd probably fell silent. All eyes turned to the woman, who Mark said came in fear and trembling and fell at the feet of the Savior to confess why she had touched him. For one terrible moment, she must have felt that the whole world had stopped, and her rejoicing must have turned to fear. What if the Lord was angry with her? What if He rebuked her boldness? And what if He took the healing away?

***

"WHO TOUCHED ME?"

***

Why would Christ delay His urgent mission with Jairus to ask that question? His custom had been to tell those He healed not to publicize the miracle. So why did He want to expose this woman to the crowd? Certainly, with His divine knowledge of all things, He knew who she was. He knew that she was already healed. He knew how urgent it was to help this Jewish ruler who had opened such an important missionary door. Why delay him?

Why bother the woman?

Why make her confess?

Why not let her go her way in peace?

But could she?

"Who touched me?" What a divine act of kindness is wrapped up in that question.

To begin with, by asking the woman to come forward, Jesus was able to eliminate any doubt or guilt she may have felt about receiving the healing deceptively. He said to her, "Daughter, be of good comfort" (Luke 8:48). Of even greater value than the healing would be the assurance that He had granted the healing willingly, knowingly. "Who touched me?" was a way to put His stamp of approval upon her faith. It was a way of showing both her and the public that she was acceptable and worthy of His notice.

A second way this question showed His kindness was by giving her the assurance that her faith in Him was valid. There was no magic in His robe. "Thy faith hath made thee whole," He said, showing that we can all use our faith with free and unrestrained agency (Luke 8:48).

Third, by asking, "Who touched me?" He was able to remove any doubt that her healing was permanent. "Go in peace, and be whole of thy plague," He said (Mark 5:34).

The fourth reason is that it removed from her the burden of proof. It would now be public knowledge that she was clean.

And the fifth and most important part of His kindness was the healing of her lonely and aching spirit. What a treasure to remember for the rest of her life—that He *knew* her; He *noticed* her; He *accepted* her! What a profound demonstration this question provides of our Savior's love, mercy, and kindness. What an exciting invitation it gives for each one of us to reach out and touch Him as well.

"WHO TOUCHED ME?"

Conclusion: How could applying the principles taught by this chapter's question help you to feel better about yourself, improve your relationship with the Lord, and lead you to greater feelings of happiness and peace?

CHAPTER SEVEN

MASTER, CAREST THOU NOT THAT WE PERISH?

And when they had sent away the multitude, they took him even as he was in the ship. And there were also with him other little ships.

And there arose a great storm of wind, and the waves beat into the ship, so that it was now full.

And he was in the hinder part of the ship, asleep on a pillow: and they awake him, and say unto him, Master, carest thou not that we perish?

And he arose, and rebuked the wind, and said unto the sea, Peace, be still. And the wind ceased, and there was a great calm.

And he said unto them, Why are ye so fearful? How is it that ye have no faith?

And they feared exceedingly, and said one to another, What manner of man is this, that even the wind and the sea obey him? (Mark 4:36–41)

"MASTER, CAREST THOU not that we perish?" This question occurred after a lengthy sermon, when Jesus asked His disciples to take Him to the other side of the Sea of Galilee. We don't know the exact size of their ship, but we do know it was a rather large fishing vessel with a mast and sail, and that it was large enough to draw Mark's contrast to "the little ships" that some of the crowd used while trying to follow them across the sea. Exhausted from His labors, the Savior found a place to rest at the stern of the ship and quickly fell asleep on a pillow.

There is great significance in that fatigue, because it demonstrates the humanness of the Savior—that He was not a superman, but actually mortal and subject to the same needs of the flesh that we have. Without food His mortal body hungered; without water He thirsted. And without sleep He tired from His labors, subject to the same fatigue that we experience. "And lo, he shall suffer temptations, and pain of body, hunger, thirst, and fatigue, even more than man can suffer, except it be unto death" (Mosiah 3:7).

As the ship made its way toward the other side, their vessel was threatened by a sudden and violent windstorm. The Sea of Galilee lies over six hundred feet below sea level and is surrounded by hills and mountains. Such storms are often created as the cooler air from above rushes down upon the warmer water, but it appears that this storm was of such ferocity that even these seasoned seamen were frightened by it. As large as the ship was, the huge waves poured into it, filling it faster than they could bail. The wind was so severe that the ship was in danger of breaking apart or sinking.

There is a parallel here to the great storms of turmoil and adversity that sometimes sweep into our own lives, emotional storms that threaten to engulf and destroy us with their disruptive and discouraging power. Too often we react to our storms as those disciples did, with doubt and fear, with distrust and, unfortunately, even with accusations against God. Realizing that they were helpless to save themselves, the disciples waded to the stern of the boat to wake the Savior, who was still peacefully asleep. They roused Him with this pitiful question: "Master, carest thou not that we perish?"

This is one of the saddest questions ever asked of the Savior, a question that, unfortunately, some of us have asked as well. It is a biting, accusatory question, perhaps one of the most painful ever hurled at Him because it came from His closest disciples, who were now expressing doubt of His love and concern for them. There was no sin in their fear. The dangers were real. But they could have said, "Lord, please wake up. We need your help," or "Lord, we're in trouble, the boat is about to sink. Can you help us? Will you save us?" But they didn't.

"MASTER, CAREST THOU NOT THAT WE PERISH?"

What this sad and very human question really asks is, "Why don't you care about our problem? Here we are trying to serve you and we are about to be destroyed. Why are you letting this happen to us?" And haven't we all questioned God in the same way during some trouble or crisis in our own lives?

"Why me, Lord?"

"What did I do to deserve this?"

"Why are you letting this happen to me?"

"Where are you when I need you? Why don't you care about what's happening to me?"

I think the Savior may have been wounded by their doubts and accusations. "Why are ye so fearful?" He asked, "How is it that ye have no faith?" (Mark 4:40). In other words, "How can you doubt my love and concern? You've been with me all these months and you have seen my compassion and concern for the suffering of my brothers and sisters. Where is your faith? When will you learn that you can trust me and count on my help in any circumstance or problem? When will you learn that my Father and I will never ignore or neglect you? That we always care about what is happening in your life? That we will never let you down. No matter what happens, we will be part of it with you, showing our compassion and love."

He arose and stilled the storm with but three words, "Peace, be still"—words that we would do well to apply to the storms in our own lives (Mark 4:39). The astonished disciples, well acquainted with the length of such storms, marveled at the miracle. "What manner of man is this, that even the wind and the sea obey him?" (Mark 4:41). It is an important question in our own discipleship. What manner of Savior do *we* know? In our times of stress, adversity, and fear, it is not *what* we know about the gospel that will sustain us, but *who* we know. Without an assurance of God's loving concern for our suffering, the experiences of life can make us hard, cold, and bitter. But if we truly know Jesus Christ as a loving and personal shepherd, if we know Him as "the God of all comfort; Who comforteth us in all our tribulation" (2 Corinthians 1:3–4), then we can have peace and joy right in the midst of even our worst difficulties.

Do we think of Christ as someone far away, someone busy with other affairs and unconcerned about our problems, or do we know Him as did Peter (who was there during this storm) and who taught that we should cast "all your care upon him; for he careth for you" (1 Peter 5:7). Do we trust Him as Alma did when he testified that "whosoever shall put their trust in God shall be supported in their trials, and their troubles, and their afflictions" (Alma 36:3)? If we feel alone, or fail to receive His comfort in the midst of our trials, we may be certain that the fault lies within ourselves, and not with an indifferent God, for "ye may know of a surety that I, the Lord God, do visit my people in their afflictions" (Mosiah 24:14).

"MASTER, CAREST THOU NOT THAT WE PERISH?"

One day as I walked down the hall at work, I noticed a woman leaning against the wall, talking to her supervisor. As I approached, I noticed tears streaming down her face, and even though I didn't know her and couldn't hear the conversation, I could see the anguish and pleading in her expression. The supervisor's face, however, was cold and unyielding.

That isn't right, I thought to myself. No matter what the problem is, even if he cannot grant her request, he could at least respond with compassion rather than with cold indifference. I wanted to interrupt. I wanted to put my arm around her and say, "I am your brother and I care. I probably can't help with your problem, but I just want you to know that I care and would help if I could." Of course the political structure of management-employee relations in today's world does not permit such intrusions.

As I contemplated that occasion, and sorrowed that this woman was going through her trial without comfort, I felt grateful to know that we have a Father in Heaven and a Savior who are perfectly aware of our problems and yearn to give us comfort and encouragement. I have glimpsed the infinite concern they have for us by realizing that if I, a mere mortal, and stranger to this woman, can be moved so deeply with feelings of concern for her, how much more must our perfect Heavenly Father and Savior feel for each of us.

"MASTER, CAREST THOU NOT THAT WE PERISH?"

So much of our sorrow comes from the mistaken belief that no one understands or cares about what we are going through. Our burdens are so much heavier when we assume that we are alone in our grief. How kindly and lovingly the Lord has tried to teach us that He always knows and that He always cares. For example, "Can a woman forget her sucking child, that she should not have compassion on the son of her womb?" He asked. Yes, He said, as unthinkable as that seems, there may be circumstances in which even a mother might forget or not care. But, He assured, even if "they may forget, yet will I not forget thee" (Isaiah 49:15).

Yet as much as the Savior longs to wrap us in the arms of His love and comfort, He is often restrained from doing so because our preoccupations prevent Him. Consider, for example, a symbolic vision in which Joseph Smith saw nine apostles in a foreign land. They had been beaten. They were tattered and discouraged, standing in a circle without shoes and looking at the ground in despair.

Standing above them in the air was the Savior, reaching toward them, yearning to comfort them, yearning to strengthen and encourage them. But they did not see Him nor discern His presence. The Savior looked upon them and wept. It is said that the Prophet could never relate this vision without weeping himself.

Speaking of Joseph's deep emotion, Truman G. Madsen asked, "Why? Why should he be so touched? Because Christ willingly came to the earth so that the Father's family could come to him boldly, knowing that he knows what is taking place in us when we sin, that he knows all our feelings and cares. The greatest tragedy of life," he said, "is that, having paid that awful price of suffering 'according to the flesh that his bowels might be filled with compassion,' (see Alma 7:11–13) and being now prepared to reach down and help us, he is forbidden because we won't let him. We look down instead of up."[1]

"MASTER, CAREST THOU NOT THAT WE PERISH?"

Conclusion: How could applying the principles taught by this chapter's question help you to feel better about yourself, improve your relationship with the Lord, and lead you to greater feelings of happiness and peace?

NOTES

1. Truman G. Madsen, *The Highest in Us* (Salt Lake City: Bookcraft, 1978), 85.

CHAPTER EIGHT

LORD, IS IT I?

And as they did eat, he said, Verily I say unto you, that one of you shall betray me.

And they were exceeding sorrowful, and began every one of them to say unto him, Lord, is it I?

And he answered and said, He that dippeth his hand with me in the dish, the same shall betray me. (Matthew 26:21–23)

AS THE EVENING of Atonement approached, during His last supper with His apostles, the Lord began to direct their awareness toward the coming events. Surely they were astonished when He declared that one of them would be responsible for betraying the Savior to His enemies. They were certainly aware of His enemies and their desire to harm or silence him, but it was unthinkable that one of *them*, one of this inner circle of disciples, was to be the traitor. These good men are to be admired and commended for their immediate expression of self-analysis, "Lord, is it I?" How much more likely it would have been for them to be looking at each other, wondering, "Is it *him*?" But instead, they earnestly inquired if this betrayal could be an unsuspected flaw within their own actions or character.

I found this probing question to be very helpful during my own times of self-reflection, such as a temple session, prayer, and the sacrament. In fact, Paul admonished caution before taking the sacrament, to "let a man examine himself," lest he partake unworthily (see 1 Corinthians 11:27–28). The self-examining question, "Lord, is it I?" reminds me of the example of the Psalmist's spiritually mature prayers, such as, "Examine me, O Lord, and prove me; try my reins and my heart" (Psalm 26:2). Or, "Search me, O God, and know my heart: try me, and know my thoughts: And

41

see if there be any wicked way in me, and lead me in the way everlasting" (Psalm 139:23–24).

"LORD, IS IT I?"

How many times have we been warned not to judge each other, and yet, as fallen men and women, we are prone to compare ourselves to others? Perhaps subconsciously we ask ourselves, "Am I spiritually ahead of that person, or behind?" It is comforting to know that the Lord's judgment of us will not be in comparison to each other, but according to our individual circumstances, desires, and works. "For I, the Lord, will judge all men according to their works, according to the desire of their hearts" (D&C 137:9), "suiting [my] mercies according to the conditions of the children of men" (D&C 46:15).

When Lehi asked his sons to go back to Jerusalem and face the frightening task of getting the brass plates from the wicked and powerful Laban, Nephi did not judge, condemn, or even compare his faith and willingness to Laman's and Lemuel's rebellious attitude. He simply said, as should we, "I will go and do" (see 1 Nephi 3:5–7). How much wiser it is to say, "I will go and do" what I can with my knowledge and faith, contributing my best without comparing it to what another could do. As Elder Dallin H. Oaks counseled, "We should not presume to exercise and act upon judgments that are outside our personal responsibilities. . . . We should limit our judgments to our own stewardships."[1]

"LORD, IS IT I?"

Alma 34:32 reminds us that "this life is the time for men to prepare to meet God," but every time we change our focus from "Lord, is it I?" to judging or comparing ourselves to others, we lose ground by misdirecting our focus from how *we* should improve to how *others* should improve. Perhaps the greatest example of this spiritual trap was illustrated by the Savior's parable about people "which trusted in themselves that they were righteous, and despised others." He said:

> Two men went up into the temple to pray; the one a Pharisee, and the other a publican.

The Pharisee stood and *prayed thus with himself,* God, I thank thee, that I am not as other men are, extortioners, unjust, adulterers, or even as this publican.

I fast twice in the week, I give tithes of all that I posses.

And the publican, standing afar off, would not lift up so much as his eyes unto heaven, but smote upon his breast, saying, God be merciful to me a sinner.

I tell you, this man went down to his house justified rather than the other: for every one that exalteth himself shall be abased; and he that humbleth himself shall be exalted. (Luke 18:9–14; emphasis added)

Of course there are times when human mistakes and flaws are obvious. Perhaps we see someone from our church rent an inappropriate movie, or we hear an untruth spoken in a class or a talk. We see a parent discipline a child in anger rather than love, we notice a typing error in the Sunday bulletin—the examples could fill volumes because we all make mistakes and we all sin. The question is not whether the flaws and improprieties we see in others are valid; the question is where our attention is focused and whether we are trying to perfect others—or ourselves. As Mark D. Chamberlain explained: "When we become preoccupied with the weaknesses of others, our attention is distracted from our own faults. We develop a kind of spiritual farsightedness, focusing our vision on faults of others, and our spiritual eyes may begin to play tricks on us as we see right through things that are much closer—our own faults."[2]

After abridging six centuries of the Nephite's cyclic suffering because of pride and disobedience, Mormon lamented, "And thus we can behold how false, and also the unsteadiness of the hearts of the children of men" (Helaman 12:1). Similarly, we learn from the brother of Jared that "because of the fall our natures have become evil continually" (Ether 3:2). "Lord, is it I?" is important to our spiritual progress because no matter how righteously we try to live, as long as we dwell in a body of mortal, fallen flesh, it is always going to be easier to sin than it will be not to sin, for as President Spencer W. Kimball warned, "Generally *the evil way is the easier,* and since man is carnal that way will triumph unless there be a conscious and a consistently vigorous effort to reject the evil and follow the good."[3]

Nephi challenged us, as we read and study the scriptures, to liken them unto ourselves (see 1 Nephi 19:24; 2 Nephi 11:8). This "Lord-is-it-I?" attitude elevates our scripture study from one of history to one of personal application. It changes our study of the scriptures from merely gaining *information* to gaining spiritual *development*. How fitting then is Paul's admonition to "examine yourselves, whether ye be in the faith" (2 Corinthians 13:5).

"LORD, IS IT I?"

Conclusion: How could applying the principles taught by this chapter's question help you to feel better about yourself, improve your relationship with the Lord, and lead you to greater feelings of happiness and peace?

NOTES

1. " 'Judge Not' and Judging," *Ensign*, August 1999, 9.
2. "The Spiritual Hazards of Faultfinding," *Ensign*, August 1996, 56.
3. Spencer W. Kimball, *The Miracle of Forgiveness* (Salt Lake City: Bookcraft, 1969), 15; emphasis added.

CHAPTER NINE

WILL A MAN ROB GOD?

Will a man rob God? Yet ye have robbed me. But ye say, Wherein have we robbed thee? In tithes and offerings. (Malachi 3:8)

———————

THERE ARE MANY ways to "rob God" besides withholding our financial contributions to His Church. We can also rob God by withholding our time and talents, or by being less than He needs us to be to effectively influence those whom He brings within our stewardship.

Ezra Taft Benson said, "You are not just ordinary young men and young women. You are choice spirits, many of you having been held back in reserve for almost 6,000 years to come forth in this day, at this time."[1] And H. Burke Peterson said, "My dear friends, you are a royal generation. You were preserved to come to the earth in this time for a special purpose. Not just a few of you, but all of you. *There are things for each of you to do that no one else can do as well as you.*"[2]

As we each seek to do those things that "no one else can do as well," it would be well to remember Paul's admonition to "be not weary in well doing" (2 Thessalonians 3:13), and also that "it is an imperative duty that we owe to *all the rising generation* . . . that we should waste and wear out our lives" in their service (D&C 123:11–13; emphasis added). Elder Neal A. Maxwell spoke of this foreordained rising generation when he taught that all members who now live on the earth were sent here at this specific time either to prepare the world for the Second Coming of Christ, or to train those who will do so—two of the most important missions ever assigned to mortal men and women. To fail to perform either of those important duties valiantly would not only rob God of the service He sent us here to give, but could possibly delay that coming. Elder Maxwell said:

We have long heard, and believed, that the Lord has reserved special spirits to come forth in the last days of the last dispensation. The Church's rising generation of young men and women are a part of that vanguard. *Reserved* by the Lord for this time, they must now be *preserved* by parents and *prepared* for their special moment in human history! They have been *held back* to come forth at this time, but now they need to be *pushed forward* to meet their rendezvous. . . .

Just as the rising generation is here, now, by divine design—so are we who have been placed just ahead of them. Our lives and theirs have and will intersect many times before it is all over, and not by accident. . . .

God bless us with a sense of being about Our Father's business and with a keen sense of trusteeship for the rising generation.[3]

When the prophets challenge us to lengthen our stride, to reach higher to withhold our time, attention, and affections from the things of the world; to live purer, to increase our devotion and serve valiantly, I would feel that I was robbing God if I did not earnestly strive to become my best and do my best in His service. As President Ezra Taft Benson said, "Not to be valiant in one's testimony is a tragedy of eternal consequence. There are members who know this latter-day work is true, but who fail to endure to the end."[4]

"WILL A MAN ROB GOD?"

One of the ways Jesus Christ will "discern between the righteous and the wicked" will be by distinguishing "between him that serveth God and him that serveth him not" (3 Nephi 24:18). It is sobering to know that He takes very personally how we serve and treat our brothers and sisters. "Inasmuch as ye have done it unto one of the least of these my brethren, ye have done it unto me," He declared, but "Inasmuch as ye did it not to one of the least of these, ye did it not unto me" (Matthew 25:40, 45). We would all agree that we would be robbing our landlord if we failed to pay an honest rent. Elder Russell C. Taylor compared our service in the kingdom to the rent we owe the Lord: "My experience teaches that the highest goodness attainable is a life of unselfish service to mankind. . . . It has been wisely said, 'Service is the rent we pay for our own room on earth.' We should know that the rent is due on a daily basis and know that the receipt is never stamped 'paid in full,' because the rent, service in God's kingdom, is due today and due tomorrow."[5]

The scriptures are replete with descriptions of how we may effectively serve each other. Let us consider just two: the way we use our hands and arms, and the way we use our mouths. Just as the Savior spent His mortal ministry using His hands and arms to touch and love His brothers and sisters, He is now seeking to continue that ministration through us. *"And their arm shall be my arm* . . . and they shall fight manfully for me" (D&C 35:14). To those who are willing to serve Him, He says, "*I will make an instrument of thee* in my hands unto the salvation of many souls" (Alma 17:11; emphasis added), and "*by your hands* I will work a marvelous work among the children of men" (D&C 18:44; emphasis added).

I remember a time during my first year away from home in a new ward. The people were unfamiliar and seemed unfriendly to me. I felt unwelcome and unwanted. Then, on what I had resolved would be my last Sunday there, a man I did not know came along beside me in the hall. Putting his arm around my shoulder as we walked, he asked who I was and invited me to an activity. I am grateful he did not rob God of the influence he had to give to someone in need. That one simple act of a disciple of Christ using his arms to "gather a lamb" helped me feel wanted and kept me attending.

"WILL A MAN ROB GOD?"

Just as the Savior spent His mortal ministry using His mouth to express love for His brothers and sisters, He is now seeking to continue that ministration through our mouths. He has promised great blessings for those who will use their mouths in His service. "Yea, open your mouths and spare not, and you shall be laden with sheaves upon your backs, for lo, I am with you" (D&C 33:9). On the other hand, it is displeasing to the Lord when His disciples rob Him of the influence He needs because they will not open their mouths in His service. "But with some I am not well pleased, for they will not open their mouths, but they hide the talent which I have given unto them, because of the fear of man. Wo unto such, for mine anger is kindled against them" (D&C 60:2).

Elder Hugh W. Pinnock told of a young girl who felt bad about herself because her family was poor and she could not dress like the other students.

Most of the students made fun of her, which is certainly a betrayal of the Savior, who taught the importance of loving and nourishing each other with our words (see Job 4:4; 6:25; Proverbs 15:1, 23; Isaiah 50:4). She felt inferior, insecure, and unimportant. But there was one boy who did not betray his discipleship. He used his mouth to treat her kindly and non-judgmentally. From time to time he would simply say hello or give her a friendly "How ya doing?" as they passed in the hall. One day the girl told the young man that he had saved her life.

"What do you mean, I saved your life?" he asked in amazement.

"Do you remember the day we had that history test and you invited me to study with you? I was going to take my life that day. I was so tired of having people make fun of the way I dress, of the way I look, the things I say. No one seemed to care. But you cared, and because of that I'm still alive."[6]

"WILL A MAN ROB GOD?"

No matter where we live, no matter where we serve, there are always people within our sphere of influence who are hungering and thirsting for the spiritual nourishment we could give them by leading their souls to Christ. We all know people who are sick at heart and imprisoned by weaknesses or bad habits they have not been able to conquer by themselves. The Lord needs us to teach each other of the Savior's healing, liberating love and the principles of spiritual transformation from the natural man to a "new creature" in Christ. But these are not gifts we can share until we have personally experienced them ourselves. Ultimately, anything we could ever *do* for God depends more on what we have *become* inwardly than on what we *do* outwardly. The greatest theft of all, then, may be choosing to accept ourselves as we are instead of stretching to become more like Christ, so that we will be prepared and qualified to give whatever He needs us to give.

A personal example of this: I struggled with addictions for over thirty years before I finally found someone prepared and qualified to teach me about the power of Jesus Christ to change my heart and set me free from that captivity. If you, the reader, had known me during those long, empty years, could the Lord have used you to rescue me by bringing me to Christ? What if the Lord needs *you* right now to be a resource and help to someone you *do* know? What if they have to continue suffering because you are not sufficiently prepared to be God's instrument, don't really care about them, or are so busy that you fail to notice?

"WILL A MAN ROB GOD?

Conclusion: How could applying the principles taught by this chapter's question help you to feel better about yourself, improve your relationship with the Lord, and lead you to greater feelings of happiness and peace?

NOTES

1. "A Message to the Rising Generation," *Ensign*, November 1977, 30.
2. "Your Life Has a Purpose," *New Era*, May 1979, 5; emphasis added.
3. "Unto the Rising Generation," *Ensign*, April 1985, 8, 11; emphasis in original.
4. "Valiant in the Testimony of Jesus," *Ensign*, February 1987, 2.
5. "The Joy of Service," *Ensign*, November 1984, 23.
6. See "Thoughts That Need Thinking," *Ensign*, October 1980, 19.

CHAPTER TEN

HOW COULD YOU HAVE FORGOTTEN YOUR GOD IN THE VERY DAY THAT HE HAD DELIVERED YOU?

And because of my mourning and lamentation ye have gathered yourselves together, and do marvel; yea, and ye have great need to marvel; yea, ye ought to marvel because ye are given away that the devil has got so great hold upon your hearts.

Yea, how could you have given way to the enticing of him who is seeking to hurl away your souls down to everlasting misery and endless wo?

O, how could you have forgotten your God in the very day that he has delivered you? (Helaman 7:15–16, 20)

MANY WHO READ this book were alive when the first men landed on the moon. It is possible that many of us may live to see the day when mankind will explore Mars. As we consider that possibility, it would be difficult to imagine astronauts landing on Mars and then forgetting to report to NASA, who sent them there. Likewise, we cannot imagine that they would while away their time in idle pursuits not related to their mission. The creator of Mars, and all of the universe, has sent us to this planet on a mission of far greater importance and yet many of us become so preoccupied with our daily affairs that we do while away our time frivolously, forgetting the God who sent us here.

Forgetting our covenants and forgetting to remember and appreciate the Lord in our daily activities is such a common failing in mankind that it is discussed in the scriptures over six hundred times! For example, "The wicked, through the pride of his countenance, will not seek after God: God is not in all his thoughts" (Psalm 10:4). Both the Book of Mormon and the Old Testament are saturated with examples of "how quick the children of men do forget the Lord their God" (Alma 46:8; also 1 Nephi 17:45). Jeremiah quoted the Lord's lament: "Can a maid forget her ornaments, or a bride her attire? yet my people have forgotten me days without number" (Jeremiah 2:32).

At the conclusion of his magnificent address about having our hearts and natures changed by Christ, King Benjamin warned of the need to be watchful of where we focus our thoughts and attention, warning, "And now, O man, remember, and perish not" (see Mosiah 4:29–30). Similarly, Moses warned, "Only *take heed* to thyself, and keep thy soul diligently, *lest thou forget* the things which thine eyes have seen, and *lest they depart from thy heart* all the days of thy life" (Deuteronomy 4:9; emphasis added).

We can understand how people can drift away, but our question is, "How could you have forgotten your God *in the very day that he has delivered you?*" There are many records of people forgetting quickly. For example, after all the unprecedented miracles by which God delivered the Israelites from bondage in Egypt, they "understood not [his] wonders in Egypt; *they remembered not the multitude of [his] mercies*; but provoked him at the sea, even at the Red sea" (Psalm 106:7; Exodus 14:11–12; emphasis added). And even after the miracle of the Red Sea parting for their miraculous deliverance, they did not remember the Lord during the forty-day absence of Moses while he received the Ten Commandments on the mountain-top. In less than six weeks, without Moses to remind them, they actually formed a graven calf and worshiped it, declaring that it was the god which had brought them out of Egypt! (see Exodus 32:7–8; Deuteronomy 9:12).

Apparently, appreciation for divine blessings, even major blessings like deliverance from captivity, does not come naturally to fallen man. "*Ye do not remember the Lord your God in the things with which he hath blessed you,*" charged Samuel, the Lamanite prophet, "but ye do always remember your riches, not to thank the Lord your God for them; yea, your hearts are not drawn out unto the Lord, but they do swell with great pride, unto boasting" (Helaman 13:22; see also 12:1–5; emphasis added).

"HOW COULD YOU HAVE FORGOTTEN YOUR GOD IN THE VERY DAY THAT HE HAS DELIVERED YOU?"

We can understand such forgetfulness because most of us have made sincere resolutions, promises, and even covenants, with full intention to keep them, but found ourselves very quickly in violation of those good intentions. This misdirected preoccupation and forgetfulness is not restricted to the wicked, but is also a struggle for even the most righteous of us.

Joseph Smith, for example, after seeing both the Father and the Son in his first vision, reported, "I frequently fell into many foolish errors, and displayed the weakness of youth, and the foibles of human nature; which, I am sorry to say, led me into divers temptations, offensive in the sight of God" (JS—H 1:28). Nine years later he was still being admonished by the Lord to remember his duties and take his prophetic role more seriously. "And now I command you, my servant Joseph, to repent and walk more uprightly before me, and to yield to the persuasions of men no more; And that you be firm in keeping the commandments wherewith I have commanded you" (D&C 5:21–22).

The brother of Jared was one of the few who possessed sufficient faith to pierce the veil and see the Lord face to face. Yet even he, like the rest of us, was distracted by the press of mortal affairs. Thus, "for the space of three hours did the Lord talk with the brother of Jared, and chastened him *because he remembered not* to call upon the name of the Lord" (Ether 2:14; emphasis added).

"HOW COULD YOU HAVE FORGOTTEN YOUR GOD IN THE VERY DAY THAT HE HAS DELIVERED YOU?"

Because of the constant barrage of contradictory things presented by this imperfect world, our faith and testimonies are in constant jeopardy and require continual renewal. When we forget the hand of the Lord in our daily lives, our faith and testimony can quickly wither and shrivel away. Thus Christ commanded us, "Let the solemnities of eternity rest upon your minds" and "look unto me in every thought" (D&C 43:34; 6:36). One might wonder if this is even possible, considering the demands of work, school, parenting, housekeeping, and all the other things that compete for our attention. Of course it is possible because we know that "the Lord giveth no commandments unto the children of men, save he shall prepare a way for them that they may accomplish the thing which he commandeth them" (1 Nephi 3:7). The Lord has commanded that we remember Him in prayer throughout the day, during all the demands of work, school, parenting, and housekeeping, and all the rest of our daily mortal affairs (see Alma 34:20–27). Remembering Him during those very activities can bring us even closer to Him.

Remembering the Lord *always* is a skill that grows with practice and determination. Like any skill development, we simply start from where we are, sharing with the Lord our desire to remember Him more attentively, asking for His help. With the assistance of the Holy Spirit, whose mission it is to "bring all things to [our] remembrance" (John 14:26), it is quite possible for all who truly desire the Lord's personal companionship to remember Him in their daily lives. The two main ways the Lord has prepared to help us develop remembering skills is through daily study of the scriptures and through honoring the covenant we make in the weekly ordinance of sacrament to win the companionship of His Spirit by remembering Him always.

Just as the strength of an electromagnet is proportionate to the amount of current passed through a bar of metal, so it is with the spiritual current of thought and memory passing through our minds. It works like a mathematical ratio. The more we learn to hold Christ in the focus of our attention, the closer we will feel to Him and the more spiritually minded, "polarized" or "magnetized," our minds will be to attract His Spirit to us. On the other hand, the less we focus on Christ and His scriptural promises, the farther away He will seem. The less we remember Him, the more room there will be for the problems, temptations, and distractions of the world to crowd into our minds and separate us from the Savior and His fellowship.

As King Benjamin verified, if we would be close to Christ, "Ye should remember to retain [His] name written always in your hearts, that ye are not found on the left hand of God, but that ye hear and know the voice by which ye shall be called. . . . For how knoweth a man the master . . . who is a stranger unto him, and is far from the thoughts and intents of his heart?" (Mosiah 5:12–13). It is not reasonable to expect to make a personal friend of someone we hardly ever think about except for a few minutes once a week in church.

The Lord is so appreciative of those with the spiritual discipline to keep the sacrament covenant of "remembering Him always" that "a book of remembrance" is being written to record "them that feared the Lord, and that thought upon his name" (3 Nephi 24:16; see also Malachi 3:16). When Christ returns, those whose names are in that record will be singled out for special greeting. "Yea, when thou comest down, and the mountains flow down at thy presence, thou shalt meet him who rejoiceth and worketh righteousness, *who remembereth thee* in thy ways" (D&C 133:44; emphasis added). But "all they who are *not* found written in the book of remembrance shall find none inheritance in that day, but they shall be cut asunder" (D&C 85:9; emphasis added).

Ammon testified that God remembers and "*is mindful* of every people, whatsoever land they may be in" (Alma 26:37; emphasis added). He is mindful of us because He is always thinking about us and pondering how He can best help us make the journey back to him. "Many, O Lord my God, are thy wonderful works which thou hast done, and *thy thoughts which are to us-ward* . . . if I would declare and speak of them, *they are more than can be numbered*" (Psalm 40:5; emphasis added).

It is awe-inspiring to realize that God's thoughts and attention are directed equally to the very least of us, for "*he remembereth every creature of his creating*" (Mosiah 27:30; emphasis added). As unworthy and undeserving as we are in our fallen condition, if God directs so much of His attention to *us*, surely we can respond to this love by keeping our thoughts clean and devoting time to remember and appreciate Him. "And now behold, I say unto you, my brethren, you that belong to this church, have you sufficiently retained in remembrance?" (Alma 5:6).

"HOW COULD YOU HAVE FORGOTTEN YOUR GOD IN THE VERY DAY THAT HE HAS DELIVERED YOU?"

Conclusion: How could applying the principles taught by this chapter's question help you to feel better about yourself, improve your relationship with the Lord, and lead you to greater feelings of happiness and peace?

CHAPTER ELEVEN

DOTH HE CRY UNTO ANY, SAYING: DEPART FROM ME?

He doeth not anything save it be for the benefit of the world; for he loveth the world, even that he layeth down his own life that he may draw all men unto him. Wherefore, he commandeth none that they shall not partake of his salvation.

Behold, doth he cry unto any, saying: Depart from me? Behold, I say unto you, Nay; but he saith: Come unto me all ye ends of the earth, buy milk and honey, without money and without price. (2 Nephi 26:24–25)

MANY OF US have faulty perceptions of God's love because we grew up in homes where our parents' love was used as a tool for discipline, given freely when we behaved properly, but withdrawn when we were naughty. God's love is not like that. The love of our Heavenly Father and Savior never fluctuates because it is perfect and therefore unwavering.

I will confess that I have often pondered the mystery of how a perfect God could love me just as I am, full of imperfection, sin, and weakness. For a long time I mistakenly believed that I had to somehow make myself good enough for God before He could accept me and love me. I have learned that His love for us is not based on how *good* we are, but rather, on *who* we are—the children of God and the brothers and sisters of Jesus Christ. With all the love of a tender and affectionate parent, God is concerned less with the mistakes we have made than He is with having our hearts made right with Him and whether our desires are righteous.

It took me a long time to discover that Christ wanted to be a part of my life by helping me to overcome the unworthiness that loomed so large in my self-perceptions. I've learned that God doesn't demand that we overcome every fault before He loves us, because He knows that if we need changing, discovering His love for us will lead us to change (see Romans 2:4).

"DOTH HE CRY UNTO ANY, SAYING: DEPART FROM ME?"

Instead of dreading a rebuff when we come to Christ, we are told that "the gate of heaven *is open unto all*, even those who will believe on the name of Jesus Christ, who is the Son of God" (Helaman 3:28; emphasis added). "Behold," said the Lord, "mine arm of mercy is extended towards you, and *whosoever will come*, him will I receive" (3 Nephi 9:14; emphasis added). Christ is so anxious to welcome us in fellowship with Him and to partner with us in our efforts to increase our spirituality that He promises, "Draw near unto me and I will draw near unto you" (D&C 88:63; also James 4:8). And as Nephi testified, "Behold, hath the Lord commanded any that they should not partake of his goodness? Behold I say unto you, Nay; but *all men* are privileged the one like unto the other, and *none are forbidden*" (2 Nephi 26:28; emphasis added).

In New Testament times there was nothing considered as repulsive and abhorrent as the leper. Everywhere he went, he was required to call out a warning, such as "Unclean, unclean. Stand clear. Don't get too close." That is exactly how Satan wants us to feel when we sin. "Unclean, unclean. Don't love me, don't respect me, and don't get involved in my life. Stand clear, unclean."

Christ was not repulsed by the lepers. Without hesitation He said the same thing to *them* that He says to *each of us* today, "Come to me." And when they came, He actually reached out and touched them! That fearless touch of love and acceptance amazed the Jews far more than the healing did. Even though we are all spiritual lepers to some degree, the scriptures teach that there is no filthiness too repulsive to separate us from the healing touch of His love, if we will only reach out and accept it, for "God commendeth his love toward us, in that, while we were yet sinners, Christ died for us" (Romans 5:8).

Whenever a person resolves to accept the invitation to draw closer to the Savior and Heavenly Father, Satan invades and bombards the person with doubts. "Perhaps the promises are true for the apostles and prophets," he whispers, "but not for the average person. Perhaps they are true for those who are near perfection, but for you? No way!" And then he floods our minds with memories of past mistakes and present imperfections in an effort to discourage us. Many have been victimized by such whisperings. With tears of sincerity they have expressed their self-abhorrent feelings:

"I feel that I am not worth salvaging."

"I feel like I am dirtying the chapel when I go to church."

"After what I have done, I have no right to ask anyone for help, especially God."

This is wrong! The Savior's love and forgiveness are bigger than any fault of which we are repentant. Our value to Him is priceless. He left His throne of glory to suffer and die for us.

No matter what mistakes a person has made, no disciple of Christ should have these self-condemning feelings. They come from Satan, not from the Savior, who stands with His arms of acceptance open wide in invitation to us. "He sendeth an invitation unto all men, for the arms of mercy are extended towards them, and he saith: Repent, and I will receive you" (Alma 5:33). As one person who was guilty of serious transgression said, "At first I felt I didn't have a right to go to church. But who has more right to be in church than a sinner who is trying to come back?"[1]

"DOTH HE CRY UNTO ANY, SAYING: DEPART FROM ME?"

Christ's purpose is not to condemn us for our weaknesses, but to strengthen and encourage us, to heal us of our infirmities and sorrows, to lift us toward His level of perfection and joy. This He can and will do if we will only permit it, for He has said, "The Son of man is come to seek and to save that which was lost," and that "joy shall be in heaven over one sinner that repenteth, more than over ninety and nine just persons, which need no repentance" (Luke 19:10; 15:7). A similar testimony from Lehi used that same theme to begin the Book of Mormon witness of the Savior: "Great and marvelous are thy works, O Lord God Almighty . . . and, because thou art merciful, thou wilt not suffer those who come unto thee that they shall perish!" (1 Nephi 1:14).

Typical of the kingdom of God are not sinless people, but repentant sinners who exercise their faith in Christ by accepting His invitation to come to Him. The Savior is a God who is "ready to pardon"; He is a kind, compassionate, merciful God who has promised, "As often as my people repent will I forgive them their trespasses against me" (Mosiah 26:30; see also Moroni 6:8), "for the Lord your God is gracious and merciful, and *will not turn away his face from you*, if ye return unto him" (2 Chronicles 30:9; emphasis added).

"DOTH HE CRY UNTO ANY, SAYING: DEPART FROM ME?"

The need for repentance is never a reason to refuse or delay the Savior's invitation to come to Him, for "he inviteth them all to come unto him and partake of his goodness; and *he denieth none that come unto him*, black and white, bond and free, male and female" (2 Nephi 26:33; emphasis added). Notice that His invitation is to *every* person. It matters not to the Lord if they are "black or white, bond or free." Even if we feel trapped in bondage to bad habits or addictions, it does not matter. As long as we are willing to come to Him in sincere repentance, we are still invited to "come unto Him and partake of his goodness."

Nowhere in the scriptures do we find the Savior's invitation extended to people who need no repentance. There is no such person. But the scriptures are full of encouragement such as "Return unto me and I will return unto you, saith the Lord of hosts" (3 Nephi 24:7), and "*blessed are they who will repent* and hearken unto the voice of the Lord their God; for these are they that shall be saved" (Helaman 12:23; emphasis added). Truly His invitations are to everyone,

Jesus Christ is not a passive Shepherd. His welcome is not only extended to all who will accept His invitation and come to Him willingly, but also to those who are timid and afraid to come. His love will always reach past our weaknesses and faults if we will only let Him into our hearts. "Behold," He said, "I stand at the door, and knock," and then He promised, "If any man hear my voice, and open the door, I will come in to him" (Revelations 3:20). President Ezra Taft Benson asked us to notice that "He does not say, 'I stand at the door and *wait for you* to knock.' He is calling, beckoning, asking that we simply open our hearts and let Him in."[2]

"DOTH HE CRY UNTO ANY, SAYING: DEPART FROM ME?"

Conclusion: How could applying the principles taught by this chapter's question help you to feel better about yourself, improve your relationship with the Lord, and lead you to greater feelings of happiness and peace?

NOTES

1. Quoted by Joy F. Evans in "From Tragedy to Hope: Helping Unwed Parents," *Ensign*, September 1985, 41.
2. "A Mighty Change of Heart," *Ensign*, October 1989, 4; emphasis added.

CHAPTER TWELVE

WHY STANDEST THOU AFAR OFF, O LORD?

Why standest thou afar off, O Lord? Why hidest thou thyself in times of trouble?

Why art thou so far from helping me, and from the words of my roaring?

O my God, I cry in the daytime, but thou hearest not; and in the night season, and am not silent.

Hide not thy face far from me . . . leave me not, neither forsake me, O God of my salvation.

Unto thee will I cry, O Lord my rock; be not silent to me. (Psalms 10:1; 22:1–2; 27:9; 28:1)

"WHY STANDEST THOU afar off, O Lord? Why hidest thou thyself in times of trouble?" Why do you seem so far away when I need You the most? "Wherefore dost thou forget us for ever, and forsake us so long time?" (Lamentations 5:20). They are questions all of us have asked.

It is quite natural to think of Christ sitting on a throne next to Heavenly Father, somewhere in heaven, separated from us by billions of light years. But Jesus Christ is not a long-distance Savior. Because of His divine power to emanate His influence throughout the universe, even when His physical presence may be elsewhere, it is as though He were right beside us, just on the other side of the veil, for Christ is "not far from every one of us" (Acts 17:27). "Mine eyes are upon you," He assured, and "*I am in your midst* [even though] ye cannot see me" (D&C 38:7; emphasis added). Through the companionship of the Holy Ghost and the promise of the sacramental covenant, He can say, like Paul, even "though

I be absent in the flesh, yet am I with you in the spirit" (Colossians 2:5; also John 14:16–17; 3 Nephi 18:7).

"*I am with you alway*, even unto the end of the world," He promised (Matthew 28:20; D&C 105:41; emphasis added). "I am with you to bless you and deliver you forever" (D&C 108:8), "a very present help in trouble" (Psalm 46:1; emphasis added). He never forgets us. He never ignores or abandons us. Not only does He promise, "I the Lord am with you, and will stand by you," but also, "I will go before your face. I will be on your right hand and on your left, and my Spirit shall be in your hearts, and mine angels round about you, to bear you up" (D&C 68:6; 84:88). Yet, in spite of such repeated assurances, "Zion said, The Lord hath forsaken me, and my Lord hath forgotten me" (Isaiah 49:14).

The Lord understands the mortal experiences that cause us to feel forsaken or to feel that God is too far away to notice or care. Perhaps that is why He said, "Am I [not] a God [close] at hand . . . and not a God afar off?" (Jeremiah 23:23). We have all experienced times when God seems to be distant, hard to reach and standing "afar off." May I suggest three reasons we might have such feelings. One is sin, another is indifference, and the third is divine testing. As to sin, the scriptures teach that it is not *God* who stands afar off or hides, but *man* who pulls away from God; it is "ye [who] do withdraw yourselves from the Spirit of the Lord, that it may have no place in you" (Mosiah 2:36; emphasis added). As Isaiah taught, "Behold, the Lord's hand is not shortened, that it cannot save; neither his ear heavy, that it cannot hear: But *your iniquities have separated between you and your God*, and your sins have hid his face from you, that he will not hear" (Isaiah 59:1–2; emphasis added).

So, while it is natural to feel distanced from the Lord and His Spirit when we are disobedient, not even our sins cause God to throw up His hands in anger or frustration. As the "God of patience" (Romans 15:5), the Lord is "full of compassion, and gracious, longsuffering, and plenteous in mercy and truth" (Psalm 86:15). Not even our mistakes or sins cause Him to abandon or forsake us. As Elder Joseph B. Wirthlin stated, "The Lord will never forsake or abandon anyone. *You* may abandon *him*, but *he will not abandon you*. You never need to feel that you are alone."[1] Even if "the mountains shall depart, and the hills be removed," Christ said, "my kindness shall not depart from thee, neither shall the covenant of my peace be removed, saith the Lord that hath mercy on thee" (Isaiah 54:10).

President George Q. Cannon said, "When we went forth into the waters of baptism and covenanted with our Father in Heaven to serve Him and keep His commandments, He bound Himself also by covenant to us that *He would never desert us, never leave us to ourselves, never forget us,* that in the midst of trials and hardships, when everything was arrayed against us, *He would be near unto us and would sustain us.*"[2]

A casual indifference on our part can easily diminish our relationship with deity, even if we are not choosing a life of sin. How could we expect to feel close to God, or have His Spirit with us, if we hardly ever think about Him except a few minutes once a week in church? Just as the Lord will not force His love upon us when we choose to sin (see 2 Nephi 26:11; D&C 1:33), He will not force His way into our lives when we choose to occupy ourselves with other priorities—even if they are not wicked.

It is not reasonable to expect to feel close to *anyone* that we take for granted. As President Kimball once explained, "I find that when I get casual in my relationships with divinity and when it seems that no divine ear is listening and no divine voice is speaking, *that I am far, far away.* If I immerse myself in the scriptures the distance narrows and the spirituality returns."[3]

"WHY STANDEST THOU AFAR OFF, O LORD?"

There is a third reason that we sometimes feel God is far away from us in spite of our efforts to remember, obey, and be close to Him, and that is divine tutoring. God said that He would test and prove us in all things (see Abraham 3:25; D&C 98:12–14; 124:55). While He never actually abandons or forsakes us, sometimes, in a loving process of divine tutoring—not unlike fasting (when our appreciation for the energy we derive from food is increased by abstinence)—experiencing His temporary withdrawal can increase our appreciation for God and His watchful care.

For example, feeling alone and abandoned in Liberty Jail, the Prophet Joseph Smith cried, "O God, where art thou? And where is the pavilion that covereth thy hiding place?" (D&C 121:1). The answer was that no matter how great our feelings of loneliness or suffering, "all these things shall give [us] experience and shall be for [our] good" (D&C 122:7). Let us remember also that even the Savior felt abandoned during His anguish on the cross: "My God, my God, why hast thou forsaken me?" (Mark 15:34; also Psalm 22:1).

"WHY STANDEST THOU AFAR OFF, O LORD?"

Perhaps these temporary feelings of emptiness are the only way we can perfect our faith and trust in His constant love and concern for us. But feeling alone and distanced from God does not mean that He is actually gone or uncaring. Just as radio waves do not disappear or dissipate because we tune to a different station, God's love and attention is always near, waiting and eager to nourish and encourage us. Our challenge is to outgrow and exchange our accusations against Him for a more mature faith and trust, even when we cannot feel Him as we desire.

However, we need to remember how skilled Satan is at recognizing the times when we feel alone and abandoned. He and his demons will be ever at our side, whispering the lie, even shouting that God has abandoned us and left us alone. "He has forgotten you," they taunt. "He is far away and doesn't care about you." If we listen to those faith-wrenching lies, we may join in crying out the classic questions, "How long wilt thou forget me, O Lord? for ever? how long wilt thou hide thy face from me?" (Psalm 13:1).

"WHY STANDEST THOU AFAR OFF, O LORD?"

The Savior's attendance to our need to feel close to Him is not passive. Speaking of the door to our hearts and emotions, He said, "Behold, I stand at the door, and knock: if any man hear my voice, and open the door, I will come in to him" (Revelation 3:20). It seems incredible that it is not the opposite. We would think He would be waiting in heaven for *us* to knock on *His* door. But instead, because of His great love for us, He comes down here, banging on the door to *our* heart, imploring, as it were, "Let me in. I want to love you. I want to heal you of your hurts and wounds. I want to help you be happy. I want to help you feel clean and stand confident before our Father. Please let me into your heart."

The tendency of the natural man, when confronted with divine promises we do not believe, is to assume they only apply to other, more worthy people. But scripture emphasizes that "he sendeth an invitation unto *all* men, for the arms of mercy are extended towards them, and he saith, Repent, and I will receive you" (Alma 5:33; emphasis added). For many years I could not believe that invitation applied to me. I was certain that because of my sins, He must have been standing very far away from me. I learned a lot about His concern and attention from the father in the parable of the prodigal son. After wasting his inheritance in riotous living and disobedience, the wayward son decided to return home. Even though it had likely been years since he left, his father, who represents our Heavenly Father, had been praying and watching hopefully for this day of return. Like our Heavenly Father and Savior, so watchful was he that even "when [his wayward son] was a great way off, his father saw him, and had compassion, and ran, and fell on his neck, and kissed him" (Luke 15:20; emphasis added).

In light of all these divine assurances that God remains near to each one of us, the question, "Why standest thou afar off, O Lord?" seems foolish indeed.

President Hinckley validated these principles when he told how he was touched by the experience of Ginger Evans, a single parent raising seven children by herself. Weighed down by the burdens of her life, she pleaded with her Father in Heaven for the privilege of coming to Him, if only for one night, to find comfort and strength for the trials to come. Tender was the answer that formed in her mind: "You cannot come to me but I will come to you." President Hinckley then observed, "No, we do not leave this life at our own will for a heavenly respite. God our Eternal Father would not have it so. But He and His Beloved Son can come to us by the power of the Spirit to comfort and sustain, to nurture and to bless."[4] This same compassion is available to each of us in our own difficulties, because the Savior has promised the faithful, "I will not leave you comfortless: *I will come to you*" (John 14:18; emphasis added).

Elder Paul H. Dunn also gave testimony that God is not hiding or standing afar off. "God the Father has not forgotten us here in mortality. He has not removed himself to a far corner of the universe to watch our antics with indifference." He said, "Many people . . . believe that he's done just that. They can't believe that he could create a universe, people a world with billions of souls, and still care a whit what happens to a single individual with his small concerns. They can't believe that they're that important to anyone, let alone to the Creator of it all. May I tell you that I know that God lives, that he cares, and that he knows each one of us individually by name."[5]

"WHY STANDEST THOU AFAR OFF, O LORD?"

Conclusion: How could applying the principles taught by this chapter's question help you to feel better about yourself, improve your relationship with the Lord, and lead you to greater feelings of happiness and peace?

NOTES

1. "Running Your Marathon," *Ensign*, November 1989, 75; emphasis added.
2. George Q. Cannon, *Gospel Truth: Discourses and Writings of George Q. Cannon*, selections by Jerreld L. Newquist (Salt Lake City: Zion's Book Store, 1957), 1:170; emphasis added.
3. Quoted by James E. Faust in "That We Might Know Thee," *Ensign*, January 1999, 4; emphasis added.
4. "To Single Adults," *Ensign*, June 1989, 74.
5. "Because I Have a Father," *Ensign*, May 1979, 8.

CHAPTER THIRTEEN

IS IT NOTHING TO YOU, ALL YE THAT PASS BY?

Is it nothing to you, all ye that pass by? Behold, and see if there be
any sorrow like unto my sorrow, which is done unto me, wherewith the
Lord hath afflicted me in the day of his fierce anger. (Lamentations 1:12)

NOTE THAT THIS verse was part of Jeremiah's lamentation over the
wickedness and punishment of ancient Jerusalem. But like so many verses
hidden in the text of the Old Testament, it contains such an obvious messianic interpretation that Handel included it in his inspired oratorio *The
Messiah*. (For examples of similarly hidden messianic prophecies, see Psalm
31:5, fulfilled in Luke 23:46; and Psalm 41:9, fulfilled in John 13:18–30.)

Have you ever experienced the feelings that come from giving an
expensive gift or an act of service that required sacrifice on your part,
only to have it go unnoticed, unappreciated, or even spurned? In addition
to all that Christ suffered from paying for our sins to open the door to
repentance and forgiveness, He was even further wounded by the indifference and confusion of the very ones He was suffering to save. Far too
many disciples have failed to give serious study to this event, taking it for
granted and failing to give it the attention and response commanded by
scripture.

As this book is preparing to go to press, our nation and much of
the world is watching the close race for the Democratic nomination for
the next president of the United States. Daily, and often hourly, TV,
newspaper, and magazine commentators devote their unceasing attention to this very first race between a candidate of black heritage, Barack
Obama, and his close competitor, Hillary Clinton. So intense is the media

coverage that it seems unlikely that there could be even one cognizant adult in America who is not only aware but keenly interested in this momentous and unprecedented event in our nation's history. And yet, regrettably, most of the world is not only unaware but even unconcerned about the most significant event ever to occur in the history of the world—the Atonement of Jesus Christ.

Elder Bruce R. McConkie said, "Nothing in the entire plan of salvation compares in any way in importance with that most transcendent of all events, the atoning sacrifice of our Lord. It is the most important single thing that has ever occurred in the history of created things; it is the rock foundation upon which the gospel and all other things rest."[1]

"IS IT NOTHING TO YOU, ALL YE THAT PASS BY?"

"I have trodden the winepress *alone*," said Christ. "I looked, and *there was none to help*; and I wondered that there was none to uphold" (Isaiah 63:3, 5; also D&C 76:107; emphasis added). In further lamentation He said, "Reproach hath broken my heart; and I am full of heaviness: and *I looked for some to take pity, but there was none*; and for comforters, but I found none" (Psalm 69:20; emphasis added). Not even His closest apostles understood what was happening, nor could they stay awake through His intense ordeal in Gethsemane. All the disciples fled when the arresting mob came for him. Peter followed the arresting mob but denied knowing Him three times that night. Throughout the nightlong examinations, throughout the beatings, scourging, mocking ridicule, and finally the crucifixion of the next day, He was alone. Truly there were no comforters for Him.

"IS IT NOTHING TO YOU, ALL YE THAT PASS BY?"

It is easy to say that if we had been there to witness His Atonement, we would have done better at showing compassion and concern. But would we? How much compassion, attention, and appreciation do we show for it today? His divine hands were pierced as they were nailed to the cross. Those scars symbolize all that He suffered for us individually and collectively. "Behold," He said, "I have graven thee upon the palms of my hands" (Isaiah 49:16). When we come to Him in repentance, He can look at those scars graven in His hands and know exactly what our sins have cost Him in suffering. And yet how often do we think of this?

Nephi prophesied that in our time there would be many who would scorn Him with such casual indifference that they symbolically trample Him under their feet. "Yea, even the very God of Israel do men trample under their feet; I say, trample under their feet but I would speak in other words—*they set him at naught*, and hearken not to the voice of his counsels" (1 Nephi 19:7; emphasis added). Isaiah lamented our lack of appreciation when He said, "They *regard not* the work of the Lord, *neither consider* the operation of his hands" (Isaiah 5:12; emphasis added). It seems to me that "setting Him at naught" or "regarding not" means taking what He did for granted, when the least we could do is to search the meanings of what He experienced and keep it foremost in our thoughts with appreciation and devotion.

"IS IT NOTHING TO YOU, ALL YE THAT PASS BY?"

Many people have suffered scourging and crucifixion. What did the Lord mean by the rest of this verse? "Behold, and see if there be any sorrow like unto my sorrow, which is done unto me, wherewith the Lord hath afflicted me in the day of his fierce anger" (Lamentations 1:12). Lest we "regard not" or fail to "consider" what He actually did for us that night in Gethsemane and on the cross the next day, let us quickly review a brief summary, that we might never be guilty of taking this for granted or "setting it at naught."

To begin with, every pain and heartache He suffered in His life and during the Atonement was undeserved. He was perfectly pure, clean, and innocent of sin. All that He suffered to make repentance and forgiveness possible was *for* us and more important, *because* of us, for "the Lord hath laid on him the iniquity of us all" (Isaiah 53:6) and "Christ also hath once suffered for sins, the just for the unjust, that he might bring us to God" (1 Peter 3:18).

The suffering of the Atonement, however, was not just for our *sins*, but also that Jesus might personally experience *every pain and heartache* that mankind would ever suffer, so that He could then personally, in His own flesh and emotions, "comprehend all things" we have experienced when we come to Him for mercy, comfort, and help (see D&C 88: 6; 122:5–8; Alma 7:11–13). As Stephen E. Robinson explained:

> All the negative aspects of human existence brought about by the Fall, Jesus Christ absorbed into himself. He experienced vicariously in Gethsemane all the private griefs and heartaches, all the physical pains and handicaps, all the emotional burdens and depressions of the human family.
>
> He knows the loneliness of those who don't fit in or who aren't handsome or pretty. He knows what it's like to choose up teams and be the last one chosen. He knows the anguish of parents whose children go wrong. He knows the private hell of the abused child or spouse. He knows all these things personally and intimately because he lived them in the Gethsemane experience.
>
> Having personally lived a perfect life, He then chose to experience our imperfect lives. In that infinite Gethsemane experience, the meridian of time, the center of eternity, he lived a billion billion lifetimes of sin, pain, disease, and sorrow.[2]

I believe that in some way that is incomprehensible to us, the Savior looked forward from Gethsemane and backward through the corridors of time and then, person by person, sin by sin, and heartache by heartache, He paid a price for us that was infinite in its totality but finite and specific in its detailed pain. "For behold, he suffereth the pains of all men, yea, the pains of every living creature, both men, women, and children, who belong to the family of Adam" (2 Nephi 9:21). Elder Marion G. Romney said of this scripture, "The suffering he undertook to endure, and which he did endure, *equaled the combined suffering of all men.*"[3] Similarly, President Ezra Taft Benson said:

> It was in Gethsemane where Jesus took on Himself the sins of the world, in Gethsemane where *His pain was equivalent to the cumulative burden of all men*, in Gethsemane where He descended below all things so that all could repent and come to Him.
>
> The mortal mind fails to fathom, the tongue cannot express, the pen of man cannot describe the breadth, depth, or height of the suffering of our Lord—or His infinite love for us.[4]

"IS IT NOTHING TO YOU, ALL YE THAT PASS BY?"

The power of the Atonement to cleanse us of our sins and to heal our spiritual wounds depends more upon our *attitude* and regard for it than it does on our *understanding* of it. In other words, its power to influence our life and lead to spiritual transformation is not dependent on a scholarly knowledge nearly so much as it is upon our response of gratitude, reverence, and awe. As President David O. McKay taught, "What you sincerely in your heart think of Christ will determine what you are, will largely determine what your acts will be."[5]

But our relationship with Christ depends not only upon *what* we think of Christ, but also upon *how often* we think of him. For example, as we struggle to make improvements in our spiritual life, if the Atonement is the last thing in our mind, if we are indifferent or inattentive to His suffering on our behalf, it is unlikely that it will have much effect on our life. One of the essential keys to drawing closer to the Savior is simply to train ourselves to think about Him more often. The more often we remember Christ, as we promise to do in the weekly sacramental covenant, the more His Spirit will be with us and the closer we will feel to Him. Thinking about Him and remembering His sacrifice in our daily lives closes the door to other preoccupations and opens the door to our hearts, welcoming Him to enter.

Have you ever tried to teach students who were not really paying attention to you? They sort of "half listen," but your effort to help them learn and grow is not very fulfilling because you know their real attention is somewhere else. Perhaps that's a little bit like God's experience with us when we ignore the Atonement.

"IS IT NOTHING TO YOU, ALL YE THAT PASS BY?"

In spite of the Lord's efforts to keep us in remembrance of Him, the scriptures repeatedly demonstrate "how quick the children of men do forget the Lord their God" (Alma 46:8). "Beware that thou forget not the Lord thy God" is a frequent command of scripture (Deuteronomy 8:11). "Can a maid forget her ornaments, or a bride her attire?" asked the Lord, "Yet my people *have forgotten me days without number*" (Jeremiah 2:32; emphasis added).

To help us overcome the very natural preoccupation with the demands of the physical world we live in, Alma urged, "Let all thy thoughts be directed unto the Lord" (Alma 37:36), and Mormon admonished, "My son, be faithful in Christ . . . and may his sufferings and death . . . rest in your mind forever" (Moroni 9:25). Similarly, Jacob said, "We would to God that . . . all men would believe in Christ, and *view his death*, and suffer his cross and bear the shame of the world" (Jacob 1:8; emphasis added). Christ himself indicated how attentive and focused we should be on the solutions He provided with His suffering when He asked us, "Look unto me in every thought [and to] *behold* the wounds which pierced my side, and also the prints of the nails in my hands and feet" (D&C 6:36–37; emphasis added).

When Isaiah prophesied that Christ would be "wounded for our transgressions" and "bruised for our iniquities," he concluded by saying that it would be "with his stripes [that] we are healed" (Isaiah 53:5). As the enormity of His vicarious suffering, symbolized by the "stripes" inflicted by the Roman scourging, becomes real and important to us, as we feel the enormity of our debt to Him, we are born anew into a spiritual union that opens the door to receive the power of the Atonement.

"Hereby perceive we the love of God, because he laid down his life for us" (1 John 3:16). It is in "perceiving" His infinite sorrow and pain for each of us that we glimpse the magnitude of His perfect love. "For as the sufferings of Christ abound in us," and "as ye are partakers of the sufferings, so shall ye be also of the consolation" (2 Corinthians 1:5, 7). But "how knoweth a man the master . . . who is a stranger unto him, and is far from the thoughts and intents of his heart?" (Mosiah 5:13).

In contrast to this chapter's heart-wrenching question are the healing and instructive words of a beloved sacrament hymn: "I think of his hands pierced and bleeding to pay the debt! Such mercy, such love, and devotion can I forget?"[6]

"IS IT NOTHING TO YOU, ALL YE THAT PASS BY?"

Conclusion: How could applying the principles taught by this chapter's question help you to feel better about yourself, improve your relationship with the Lord, and lead you to greater feelings of happiness and peace?

NOTES

1. Bruce R. McConkie, *Mormon Doctrine*, 2nd ed. (Salt Lake City: Bookcraft, 1966), 60.
2. Stephen E. Robinson, *Believing Christ* (Salt Lake City: Deseret Book, 1992), 122–23.
3. In Conference Report, October 1969, 57, as quoted by President Howard W. Hunter in "The Opening and Closing of Doors, *Ensign*, November 1987, 59; emphasis added.
4. "Five Marks of the Divinity of Jesus Christ," *New Era*, December 1980, 47; emphasis added.
5. "Developing Character," *Ensign*, October 2001, 22.
6. "I Stand All Amazed," *Hymns of The Church of Jesus Christ of Latter-day Saints* (Salt Lake City: The Church of Jesus Christ of Latter-day Saints, 1985), 193.

CHAPTER FOURTEEN

WHY SHOULD I YIELD TO SIN, BECAUSE OF MY FLESH?

> O then, if I have seen so great things, if the Lord in his condescension unto the children of men hath visited men in so much mercy, why should my heart weep and my soul linger in the valley of sorrow, and my flesh waste away, and my strength slacken, because of mine afflictions?
>
> And why should I yield to sin, because of my flesh? Yea, why should I give way to temptations, that the evil one have place in my heart to destroy my peace and afflict my soul? . . .
>
> Awake, my soul! No longer droop in sin. Rejoice, O my heart, and give place no more for the enemy of my soul. (2 Nephi 4:26–28)

IN OUR PREMORTAL life, Satan failed to win us to his side while we were yet spirits. Now that we are here in physical bodies of fallen flesh, carnal bodies that continually opt for the lower road, Satan focuses his attacks on the misuse of our bodies. It appears that in his miserable existence, one of Satan's greatest pleasures is the victory he achieves when he persuades us to misuse our bodies. As "he seeketh that all men might be miserable like unto himself," he not only "goeth up and down, to and fro in the earth, seeking to destroy the souls of men," but he also seeks to "hurl away [our] souls down to everlasting misery and endless wo?" (2 Nephi 2:27; D&C 10:27; Helaman 7:16).

In addition to the enticements of Satan and his demons, we also face the continual downward pull of the carnal, fallen flesh, "for the flesh lusteth against the Spirit, and the Spirit against the flesh: and these are contrary the one to the other: *so that ye cannot do the things that ye would*"

(Galatians 5:17; emphasis added). "Why should I yield to sin, because of my flesh?" We yield because it gives us pleasure and because it is easier to give in than to resist. But how "can ye think of being saved when you have yielded yourselves to become subjects to the devil?" (Alma 5:20). Satan's strategy for using our bodies to defeat us is based on the immediacy of physical pleasure. As President Spencer W. Kimball said: "Evil and good influences will be ever present. One must choose. Generally, *the evil way is the easier*, and since man is carnal, that way will triumph unless there be a conscious and a consistently vigorous effort to reject the evil and follow the good."[1]

Whether we spend our mortality in bodies that are temples or addictive prisons depends largely on the way we respond to our desires. As the brother of Jared said, "Now behold, O Lord . . . we know that thou art holy . . . and that we are unworthy before thee [and that] because of the fall *our natures have become evil continually*" (Ether 3:2; emphasis added). Because we now live in physical bodies that are strange and unfamiliar to us, bodies that are carnal and lazy, Peter implored, "I beseech you as strangers and pilgrims, abstain from fleshly lusts, *which war against the soul*" (1 Peter 2:11; emphasis added).

We all wish we were perfect and above the temptations of the flesh. If we remain faithful in the battle, that day will come. But meanwhile, as we work toward that glorious day of total victory, we must not defeat ourselves with misguided feelings of self-condemnation simply because we are tempted to sin. The fact that evil sometimes appeals to us does not prove that we are unworthy, only that we are normal. That is why Christ encouraged every disciple, "Pray always lest that wicked one have power in you, and remove you out of your place" (D&C 93:49). It is important to learn that God does not reject or condemn us because we have mortal weaknesses, but invites us to come to Him for a new heart and transformation of character. "Feeling the power of Satan does not make you evil. . . . The fact that you're struggling does not mean that you are in his power or that the Spirit of God is not also striving with you. Evil consists, not of *recognizing temptation*, but of *yielding* to it."[2]

It is by the resistance and conquest of temptations that we become holy. The more we resist, the more Christlike we become. As President Kimball said, "The difference between the good man and the bad man is not that one had the temptations and the other was spared them. It is that one kept himself fortified, and resisted temptation and the other placed himself in compromising places and conditions and rationalized the situation."[3]

"WHY SHOULD I YIELD TO SIN, BECAUSE OF MY FLESH?"

An important key to fighting this battle between our righteous desires and the downward pull of Satan and our fallen flesh is to recognize the separation between our body and the eternal spirit that lives inside. Until the day of resurrection, when you become "inseparably connected," your body of flesh is not *you*; it is a suit you wear (see D&C 93:33). Think of your physical body as something separate from you—like a spacesuit worn by your spirit in this foreign environment of mortality. An astronaut would never confuse his spacesuit with his personal identity. He is aware at all times that the spacesuit he wears is merely a covering for the real person inside. And so it is with our physical bodies. Upon death you will temporarily discard that suit as surely as an astronaut sheds his spacesuit when his mission is completed.

The spacesuit is a servant to the astronaut, not the master. In the same way, our bodies should be our servants, not our masters. As Nephi asked, "And why should *I* [that is, *me*, the spirit entity inside the body] yield to sin, because of my flesh? Yea, why should *I* give way to temptations, that the evil one have place in my heart to destroy my peace and afflict my soul?" (2 Nephi 4:27; emphasis added). We also see this scriptural clarification of the conflict between our chosen path and the fallen, carnal desires of the flesh in Paul's words, "Let not sin therefore reign in your mortal body, that *ye* should obey *it* in the lusts thereof" (Romans 6:12; emphasis added). Notice that Paul did not say, "Don't give in to *your* lustful desires." He was urging us to recognize the separation much the same as Melvin J. Ballard did: "The greatest conflict that any man or woman will ever have . . . will be the battle that is had with self. I should like to speak of spirit and body as 'me' and 'it.' 'Me' is the individual who dwells in this body, who lived before I had such a body, and who will live when I step out of the body. 'It' is the house I live in, the tabernacle of flesh; and the great conflict is between 'me' and 'it.' "[4]

"WHY SHOULD I YIELD TO SIN, BECAUSE OF MY FLESH?"

The "awfulness of yielding to the enticings of that cunning one" (2 Nephi 9:39) is that the more often we yield to him, the stronger his influence becomes until he binds us in captivity and addiction. Whether we yield to temptations deliberately or only unintentionally through weakness, we are nevertheless in danger of being "*taken captive* by the devil, and led by his will down to destruction" (Alma 12:11; emphasis added). As Melvin J. Ballard said, "Secret weaknesses and vices leave an open door for the enemy of your soul to enter, and he may come in and take possession of you, *and you will be his slave*."[5]

"WHY SHOULD I YIELD TO SIN, BECAUSE OF MY FLESH?"

A major reason we came to this earth school was for our spirits to learn how to control and use a physical body to produce joy and increased capacities instead of succumbing to its captivity and restrictions. Each choice we make for the way we use our time and our bodies either leads us upward toward greater spirituality, freedom, and self-mastery, or downward toward enslavement and sorrow. This mortal probation is, in large measure, an endurance test to see if we can dwell inside a mortal body of fallen flesh without becoming slaves to it. It is a test to see which will win, our flesh or our spirit, the will of the body or the will of the person.

Paul emphasized the importance of not yielding to the sinful desires of our bodies when he said, "Put ye on the Lord Jesus Christ, and *make not provision for the flesh*, to fulfill the lusts thereof" (Romans 13:14; emphasis added). "Making provision" means arranging our time and affairs so that we can yield to unworthy desires. Not "making provision" means facing the reality of the inappropriate desires of our house of flesh and planning strategies that will reduce or eliminate the temptations and opportunities to succumb.

Each time we "make provision" and give in to evil enticements to use our bodies in ways that are not appropriate, we open ourselves to the influence of Satan's demon tempters as surely as if we had posted a welcome sign. The demons we invite into our lives are highly skilled in helping us perpetuate those choices until we reach the point of enslavement and lose our agency. "It is," said Elder Richard G. Scott, "as though Satan ties strings to the mind and body so that he can manipulate one like a puppet."[6]

"WHY SHOULD I YIELD TO SIN, BECAUSE OF MY FLESH?"

How long would you wear a pair of shoes that forced you to go where *they* chose to go rather than where *you* wanted to go? How would you like to live in a house that made up its own mind when the windows or doors would be open or shut, when the lights should be on or off, whether the temperature should be cooled or warmed? Silly, isn't it? Yet how many of us allow the natural desires and passions of our house of flesh to dictate where we go, what we feel, what we eat or drink, what we watch or do—to our everlasting damnation? Paul's important admonition was: "Neither yield ye your members as instruments of unrighteousness unto sin: but yield yourselves unto God, as those that are alive from the dead, and your members as instruments of righteousness unto God" (Romans 6:13).

"WHY SHOULD I YIELD TO SIN, BECAUSE OF MY FLESH?"

Conclusion: How could applying the principles taught by this chapter's question help you to feel better about yourself, improve your relationship with the Lord, and lead you to greater feelings of happiness and peace?

NOTES

1. *The Miracle of Forgiveness*, 15; emphasis added.
2. Don Norton, quoted in "I Have a Question," *Ensign*, August 1978, 33; emphasis added.
3. *The Miracle of Forgiveness*, 231–32.
4. "Struggle for the Soul," *New Era*, March 1984, 35; emphasis added.
5. "Struggle for the Soul," *New Era*, March 1984, 38; emphasis added.
6. "We Love You—Please Come Back," *Ensign*, May 1986, 10–11.

CHAPTER FIFTEEN

IF THE LORD BE WITH US, WHY THEN IS ALL THIS BEFALLEN US?

And there came an angel of the Lord, and sat under an oak which was in Ophrah, that pertained unto Joash the Abi-ezrite: and his son Gideon threshed wheat by the winepress, to hide it from the Midianites.

And the angel of the Lord appeared unto him, and said unto him, The Lord is with thee, thou mighty man of valour.

And Gideon said unto him, Oh my Lord, if the Lord be with us, why then is all this befallen us? and where be all his miracles which our fathers told us of, saying, Did not the Lord bring us up from Egypt? but now the Lord hath forsaken us, and delivered us into the hands of the Midianites.

And the Lord looked upon him, and said, Go in this thy might, and thou shalt save Israel from the hand of Midianites: have not I sent thee? (Judges 6:11–14)

ASKING WHY BAD things happen to people who are trying to do what is right is a good question. But it is seldom the right question—if our goal is to move forward and rise above the unwanted circumstance. If we are going to demand an accounting of why bad things happen to us, then shouldn't we also be asking why good things happen?

We cannot blame Gideon for asking, "If the Lord be with us, why then is all this befallen us?" His nation was in deep trouble and their suffering was severe.

Because of Israel's wickedness, the Lord had allowed the Midianites to plague Israel. Just as the Lamanites were allowed to invade the Nephites during their times of wickedness, just as famines and other pestilences are often sent by a loving Heavenly Father to help people and nations repent, this evil had come upon Israel because of their disobedience and refusal to repent. For years the Midianites had invaded, coming as "grasshoppers for multitude," destroying their livestock, crops, and vineyards, leaving no sustenance for the people (see Judges 6:1–5).

Finally, after seven years of suffering, the people of Israel began to get the Lord's point and humbled themselves enough for the Lord to send help. An angel was sent to raise up a man to deliver them from bondage. His name was Gideon, and while he had never participated as a leader in Israel's politics, the Lord knew the integrity of his heart. The angel messenger called him a "mighty man of valour" and said, "The Lord is with thee" (Judges 6:12).

Gideon had not seen any evidence that the Lord was with his people and asked why "the Lord hath forsaken us, and delivered us into the hands of the Midianites" (Judges 6:13). "If the Lord be with us," he challenged, "why then is all this befallen us? and where be all his miracles which our fathers told us of, saying, Did not the Lord bring us up from Egypt?" (Judges 6:13).

This challenge by a good man raises the questions asked by millions of confused disciples. "I'm trying to do what is right, so why has this happened to me?" Or, "What did I do to deserve this?" Asking *why* bad things happen to good people is the wrong question because it unproductively directs our attention to the past instead of to what we should do now in response to the situation. You cannot live one moment in the future and you cannot live one moment in the past. Unlike VCRs, which we use to watch other people living their lives, real life has no rewind or fast-forward buttons. You cannot undo or change what was done in the past, and you can only change your future by changing your present.

So the angel ignored Gideon's natural-man question of *why* and redirected his attention to the more pertinent question of *how to respond.* "And the [angel of the] Lord looked upon him, and said, Go in this thy might, and thou shalt save Israel from the hand of the Midianites: have not I sent thee?" (Judges 6:14).

"IF THE LORD BE WITH US, WHY THEN IS ALL THIS
BEFALLEN US?"

This question improperly implies that "if God be with us" nothing bad is ever going to happen to us, but in this fallen, imperfect world, that is just not realistic. Bad things happen to all people. The suffering of Gideon's countrymen was deserved and sent by a loving God as a tutoring lesson in hope of motivating their repentance, but we must not mistakenly conclude that all suffering comes from God as punishment for sin. Some of the adversity we experience is brought into our lives by our own unwise choices; some of it is inflicted upon us by improper and evil choices of others who misuse their agency. Many unwanted circumstances come simply from living in the environment of this imperfect and fallen world.

It helps to know that adversity is not something that happens *to* you. It is something that happens *for* you. We fought a premortal war for the privilege of coming here to learn from adversity and opposition. Whatever the source of our difficulties, when we are unhappy or suffering from unwanted, even undeserved or unjust, circumstances the path to freedom, peace, and victory over those circumstances lies not in demanding to know why, but in turning to the Lord's promises of the good He can and will bring out of those situations—if we will allow it.

Lehi said that the Lord is so determined to help us learn the lessons we need here that He "shall *consecrate* thine afflictions for thy gain" (2 Nephi 2:2; emphasis added). This principle was confirmed when the Lord promised, "All things wherewith you have been afflicted shall work together for your good" (D&C 98:3; see also D&C 90:24; 100:15; 122:7; Romans 8:28). Such promises have been repeated so many times that one could actually debate whether it is even possible for something "bad" to happen to us. For example, Brigham Young taught, "Every trial and experience you have passed through is necessary for your salvation."[1]

Since our problems are designed to be our teachers in this life, resenting the mortal lessons that are "necessary" for our salvation would be like paying a huge tuition to go to college and then resenting the homework. Or having such a lack of faith in the educational process that we stomp our feet over every task assigned, demanding to know why we have been given the assignment.

"IF THE LORD BE WITH US, WHY THEN IS ALL THIS BEFALLEN US?"

Everything in mortal life is a test. We know that test results are often based on our *attitude* as much as our *aptitude*. In this imperfect world of imperfect people who often make wrong choices, we can seldom choose the obstacles we must face. But no matter what happens to us, we can always choose whether we will allow unwanted circumstances to discourage and pull us down, or whether we will use them to lead us to a closer relationship with our Savior.

Paul was referring to our attitude about adversity when he taught that "no chastening for the present seemeth to be joyous, but grievous: nevertheless afterward it yieldeth the peaceable fruit of righteousness unto them which are *exercised* thereby" (Hebrews 12:11). *Exercise* is an interesting word to be attached to our tutoring adversities. The Greek translation of *exercised* means to be "trained or disciplined by the experience." Whether we will be "exercised" by our adversities, whether we will be trained, grow and profit from them, or whether our faith and testimony will be diminished depends not on *what happens to us*, but on *how we respond*. We can respond with negative emotions of doubt and resentment, which are typified by the "Why-is-God-doing-this-to-me?" questions, or with a positive expectation and trust for the good we know God will bring out of it, even if we never figure out the answer to the questions of why it happened.

Ardeth G. Kapp said, "There will be some steep climbs ahead, but our Lord and Savior Jesus Christ has covenanted and promised to climb with each of us every step of the way."[2] How could we ever know or feel that He is with us if we allow the unwanted circumstance to fill us with bitterness, anger, and resentments that are typified by the question, "If the Lord be with us, why then is all this befallen us?" Whining, wringing our hands in response to adversity, stomping our feet, and demanding an accounting of why it happened so distracts us from the growth the situation could have provided, that we make it very difficult for Him to be with us or help us to get past the pain to find the good.

One of the most powerful scriptures about trusting God during adversity comes from Job, who certainly did not deserve the unjust things that befell him. He could not make any sense of why all those horrible things were happening to him, but instead of turning bitter toward God, or becoming debilitated by the questions of *why*, he said these magnificent words: "Though he slay me, yet will I trust in him" (Job 13:15). How could he say that after all the unexplained tragedies he experienced? It is because he knew that no matter what happened to him, the Lord loved him, and that was more important to him than any suffering he could experience.

In our times of great adversity, as we struggle to just hang on, it is not *what* we know about the gospel, or *why* something happened, that will sustain us, but *whom* we know. Knowing the answer to every question of *why*, would deprive us of the opportunity to apply faith and trust. Do we trust the God who always knows what is happening, a God who is always in control of events and who is working to bring good out of what appears to be a disadvantage? Or must we forfeit the growth it could have given us by shouting, screaming, and demanding an accounting for why this is happening? If we cannot trust Him during our difficulties, then how can we claim to trust Him in anything?

Once when I was sitting at the dinner table with our eight children, one of them, still in diapers, was under the table. When I saw that she was about to stand up and bump her head, I put out my hand and cushioned the impact. She went her way completely unaware of the intervention that had saved her from pain. If we truly know Jesus Christ as our personal Shepherd, if we truly love and trust Him to be watching over our daily lives, either protecting us from unneeded pain, or bringing a compensating benefit that "works to our good," then we can have peace and joy right in the midst of our worst difficulties. We will no longer be tormented by the question:

"IF THE LORD BE WITH US, WHY THEN IS ALL THIS BEFALLEN US?"

Conclusion: How could applying the principles taught by this chapter's question help you to feel better about yourself, improve your relationship with the Lord, and lead you to greater feelings of happiness and peace?

NOTES

1. Brigham Young, *Discourses of Brigham Young*, selected and arranged by John A. Widtsoe (Salt Lake City: Deseret Book, 1961), 345.
2. "A Time For Hope," *Ensign*, November 1986, 89.

CHAPTER SIXTEEN

WHO AM I, SAITH THE LORD, THAT HAVE PROMISED AND HAVE NOT FULFILLED?

> Who am I, saith the Lord, that have promised and have not fulfilled?
>
> I command and men obey not; I revoke and they receive not the blessing.
>
> Then they say in their hearts: This is not the work of the Lord, for his promises are not fulfilled. But wo unto such, for their reward lurketh beneath, and not from above. (D&C 58:31–33)

BECAUSE WE ARE so prone to change *our* minds and break *our* promises, it is natural for us to doubt the Lord's promises. Perhaps that is why the Lord has repeatedly given assurance that He always means what He says and that we can count on Him to fulfill His word exactly as we find it in scripture. He said, for example, "I, the Lord, declare unto you, and *my words are sure and shall not fail*" (D&C 64:31; emphasis added), "for *I will fulfil my promises* which I have made unto the children of men" (2 Nephi 10:17; emphasis added). As "I have spoken it," the Lord declared, "*I will also bring it to pass*" (Isaiah 46:11; emphasis added), "and as the words have gone forth out of my mouth *even so shall they be fulfilled*" (D&C 29:30; emphasis added).

"WHO AM I, SAITH THE LORD, THAT HAVE PROMISED AND HAVE NOT FULFILLED?"

We can be certain that as we try to believe and apply the Lord's scriptural promises to our lives, Satan will be at our side, trying to make us doubt God. He will shout at us that God is a fraud, that He lies and exaggerates, that His principles and promises might work for others, but not for us. Satan, who chose to believe that God's word and plan would not work, tries constantly to dissuade our belief as well.

Christ has testified, "I, the Lord, promise the faithful and *cannot* lie" (D&C 62:6; emphasis added), and "as I, the Lord God, liveth, even so *my words cannot return void*, for as they go forth out of my mouth *they must be fulfilled*" (Moses 4:30; emphasis added). Alma said, "The decrees of God are *unalterable*," and Amulek testified, "It is *impossible* for him to deny his word" (Alma 41:8; Alma 11:34; emphasis added). How comforting it is to know that "his purposes fail not, neither are there any who can stay his hand," because "he hath all power unto the fulfilling of all his words" (D&C 76:3; 1 Nephi 9:6).

Every time we obey God's law, every time we make claim upon a promise that we find in His words, our faith and confidence in Him is strengthened. He gave His promises to encourage us to come to Him and draw upon His power and love, and He is prepared to deliver exactly as He has promised. Yet many times His promises are not fulfilled as we expect. If "he fulfilleth the words which he hath given, and he lieth not" (3 Nephi 27:18), then how can this happen? Whenever we perceive a failure to receive the fulfillment of a scriptural promise, we may be certain that the fault never lies with the principle or the promise, but somehow, within our doubt or our disobedience. For example, "Ye endeavored to believe that ye should receive the blessing which was offered unto you; but behold, verily I say unto you there were fears in your hearts, and verily this is the reason that ye did not receive" (D&C 67:3).

"WHO AM I, SAITH THE LORD, THAT HAVE PROMISED AND HAVE NOT FULFILLED?"

Since the laws "upon which all blessings are predicated" were "irrevocably decreed in heaven before the foundations of this world" (D&C 130:20), the responsibility for the flow of blessings from heaven rests upon us and not upon God. Only by failing to fulfill the requirements associated with God's blessings can we prevent His mercy and grace from flowing into our lives. His principles and promises always work—if we apply them properly.

"For all who will have a blessing at my hands shall abide the law which was appointed for that blessing, and the conditions thereof, as were instituted from before the foundation of the world" (D&C 132:5; see also 130:20–21).

Hence, if we qualify through obedience and faith, the blessings will flow. If we disobey, our violation of the law restrains God's ability to bless us, for "I, the Lord, am bound when ye do what I say; but when ye do not what I say, ye have no promise" (D&C 82:10). For example, we read of ancient Israel preventing the Lord from blessing them because of their disobedience. "Yea, they turned back and tempted God, and *limited the Holy One of Israel*" (Psalm 78:41; emphasis added).

Elder Glen L. Rudd said, "Faith is simply knowing that the Lord is there and that He will keep His promises to those who humbly approach Him."[1] Whenever we feel that His promises are not working for us, we must stop shaking our fists at the heavens and accusing God of defaulting on His promises, because it will always be inside our own hearts that we find the cause.

"WHO AM I, SAITH THE LORD, THAT HAVE PROMISED AND HAVE NOT FULFILLED?"

Christ is so anxious for us to enjoy the fulfillment of His promises that He has actually challenged us to test and prove Him if He will not fulfill His words exactly as promised (see Malachi 3:10). When we put His words to the test, He will prove that He does not lie or exaggerate, "for the word of God must be fulfilled" (Alma 5:58), and "he proveth all his words" (2 Nephi 11:3).

The Savior sent His word to change our lives, and if we will receive the promises, His words shall not return to Him void but will be fruitful in blessing us with the transformations He intended to accomplish. He said, "So shall my word be that goeth forth out of my mouth: it shall not return unto me void, but it shall accomplish that which I please, and it shall prosper in the thing whereto I sent it" (Isaiah 55:11). Not only can we place unqualified trust in every promise we read in God's word, but we may also expect to have them personally confirmed by having them fulfilled in our own experience, for "whosoever shall believe in my name, doubting nothing, *unto him will I confirm all my words*, even unto the ends of the earth" (Mormon 9:25; emphasis added). As President N. Eldon Tanner said, "All I can do is take him at his word . . . he did not say anything he did not mean. He made no promise that he is not prepared to keep."[2]

If you have difficulty believing a promise you find in the scriptures, if the overwhelming circumstances of your present defeat make the promise seem impossible, try placing your faith in the Savior, who made the promise. Jesus Christ put His honor and integrity on the line when He said, "I cannot deny my word," and "What I the Lord have spoken, I have spoken, and I excuse not myself; and though the heavens and the earth pass away, my word shall not pass away, but shall all be fulfilled" (D&C 39:16; 1:38).

"WHO AM I, SAITH THE LORD, THAT HAVE PROMISED AND HAVE NOT FULFILLED?"

Conclusion: How could applying the principles taught by this chapter's question help you to feel better about yourself, improve your relationship with the Lord, and lead you to greater feelings of happiness and peace?

NOTES

1. "Keeping the Gospel Simple," *Ensign*, January 1989, 71.
2. *Outstanding Stories by General Authorities*, compiled by Leon R. Hartshorn (Salt Lake City: Deseret Book, 1970), 209.

CHAPTER SEVENTEEN

WHO HATH PUT WISDOM IN THE INWARD PARTS?

Who hath put wisdom in the inward parts? or who hath given understanding to the heart? (Job 38:36)

———————

WISDOM IN THE inward parts of our physical bodies may refer to the intelligence that God has placed within the brain and cellular structure of our glands and organs. It is a divine programming that enables our bodies to provide us with a living tabernacle that functions almost automatically while we, the inhabitants of the physical body, go about the business of our mortal probation.

Consider our physical brains, for example, which Heavenly Father designed and created to be capable of operating our complex tabernacle on its own, automatically, with very little conscious thought on our part. Do you wish to run, or jump, or walk into another room? You simply choose the action you want (with your spirit mind) and your physical brain takes over, controlling hundreds of muscles to propel your body and maintain proper balance, leaving your mind free to think about other things. And if you do choose to run, you (the spirit being inside the body) will not need to consciously instruct your brain to make all the necessary adjustments, like accelerating the heartbeat or breathing rates, because it will do that for you.

Although it only weighs about three pounds (a very small part of the entire body mass), the brain actually uses about 20 percent of the body's blood and energy and 20 percent of all the nutrition we feed our bodies. This is remarkable when we realize the brain has no energy-hungry muscles. Keeping our body running properly requires fuel, and the brain's consumption of energy is more or less constant, whether we are concentrating or sleeping.

"WHO HATH PUT WISDOM IN THE INWARD PARTS?"

These marvelously engineered bodies contain about 75 trillion cells that differ vastly in their size, shape, and function. It has been estimated that about 200 billion of these cells become ineffectual and die every hour! But in a healthy body, these dying, worn out cells are replaced by new ones without our even being aware of the process.

To help accomplish all that it must do, the body is filled with tens of thousands of sensors that monitor bodily functions and help the brain automatically adjust things like blood pressure and body temperature, as well as the chemical level of vital substances like sugar, oxygen, and carbon dioxide in the blood. These sensors are connected to the brain by a network of over 90,000 miles of nerves. If stretched end to end, these nerves could cross back and forth across the United States of America over thirty times! Every moment there are millions of signals speeding through the body as the sensors and nerve cells go about their business of signaling the brain with the information necessary to keep the body functioning properly. Because of the data transmitted by these nerves, it has been estimated that the brain may receive as many as 100 million sensations every second!

Meanwhile, whether we think about it or not, the heart we often take for granted is pumping our blood about seventy times every minute. From before we are born until the moment we die, our heart muscles contract and relax, over and over again, forcing the blood to surge under pressure into the arteries, to be dispersed throughout the body to feed and nourish over three trillion cells. The heart pumps with such power that it may take less than a minute for your blood to circulate through some 60,000 miles of blood vessels, most of which are tiny capillaries with a diameter about thirty times smaller than a human hair. Because of the "wisdom" God has placed "in the inward parts," over 1,000 times a day the heart sends each blood cell on this journey with no thought on our part, so that every cell in the body can receive nourishment and oxygen and have its waste materials carried away.

"WHO HATH PUT WISDOM IN THE INWARD PARTS?"

In order to keep the exposed surface of the eyeball moist and protected from bacteria, our eyelids blink automatically every two to ten seconds. That's between 5,000 and 28,000 times a day! Aren't you glad you don't have to consciously remember to do that?

Cut your finger and it heals itself. Put food in your stomach and the body knows how to digest it and convert it to energy. Your brain has been programmed to respond to the multitude of different foods you may place in your stomach and initiate any of millions of chemical responses to transform those substances into the energy you need.

This vast complexity of intricate and interwoven details of the design and function of our physical body was all conceived and planned by God before we were created. "Thine eyes did see my substance, yet being unperfect; and in thy book all my members were written, which in continuance were fashioned, when as yet there was none of them" (Psalm 139:16). As Paul said, "But now hath God set the members every one of them in the body, as it hath pleased him" (1 Corinthians 12:18).

"WHO HATH PUT WISDOM IN THE INWARD PARTS?"

"There is a spirit in man," said Job (Job 32:8), and of course that is true, but it would be more accurate to say that "man *is* [a] spirit" (D&C 93:33; emphasis added), or that he has an eternal spirit living inside the body of flesh.

John's witness of God was mistranslated to say that "God *is* a Spirit" (John 4:24; emphasis added), which is true, but is not the whole truth. It would be more accurate to say that as "the God of the spirits of all flesh" (Numbers 16:22) and "the Father of spirits" (Hebrews 12:9), God, like man, *has* a spirit in addition to His tangible, physical body (see D&C 130:22). As King Benjamin said, Christ "shall come down from heaven . . . and shall *dwell in* a tabernacle of clay [mortal flesh]" (Mosiah 3:5; emphasis added). Christ later substantiated this separation between spirit and the outer body when He said, "I was in the world and *made flesh my tabernacle*, and dwelt among the sons of men" (D&C 93:4; emphasis added).

This means that when we look in a mirror, the image we see looking back is not the real us. It is a physical body, a covering that we, the spirit offspring of God, are wearing, much like the spacesuit an astronaut wears to cover and safeguard his body inside the suit. Thus we read,

"Thou hast *covered me* [that is, the spirit] in my mother's womb" (Psalm 139:13; emphasis added). The physical body God has "covered" us with is a marvel of engineering unequaled by any other creation we know of. Truly, "I am fearfully and wonderfully made" (Psalm 139:14).

"WHO HATH PUT WISDOM IN THE INWARD PARTS?"

Every ten seconds the world's population increases by 27 people.[1] That is well over 200,000 spirits a day who come here to be "covered" with physical bodies and learn how to return to Heavenly Father. How grateful we should be for the wisdom and intelligence that God has placed "in the inward parts" of our brain, glands, and organs, enabling them to run the system for us, the spirit entities within, automatically, so that we can occupy our conscious thoughts with the lessons of mortality and progressing toward exaltation. Imagine how our mortal schooling would be hampered if we had to use the majority of our time each day in monitoring and directing the operation and maintenance of our physical bodies.

Heavenly Father is the supreme intelligence in the universe. He is perfection, the ultimate of all that can be, both physically and spiritually. Our precious physical bodies are sacred, and are to be respected and reverenced as temples, if for no other reason than they are created "in the image of his own body, male and female" (Moses 6:9). As Paul emphasized, "The temple of God is holy, *which temple ye are*" (1 Corinthians 3:17; emphasis added), and "I beseech you therefore, brethren, by the mercies of God, that ye present your bodies a living sacrifice, holy, acceptable unto God, *which is your reasonable service*" (Romans 12:1; emphasis added).

"WHO HATH PUT WISDOM IN THE INWARD PARTS?"

Conclusion: How could applying the principles taught by this chapter's question help you to feel better about yourself, improve your relationship with the Lord, and lead you to greater feelings of happiness and peace?

NOTES

1. "From the Editor," *National Geographic Magazine*, October 1998, editorial page.

CHAPTER EIGHTEEN

IF GOD BE FOR US, WHO CAN BE AGAINST US?

What shall we then say to these things? If God be for us, who can be against us? (Romans 8:31)

WHEN WE ACCEPTED Heavenly Father's plan for mortal probation in this earth school, we agreed to His explanation that the tutoring we come here for would require "an opposition in all things" (see 2 Nephi 2:10–15). But now that we are here, taking the blows and learning the lessons of mortality, we sometimes become discouraged and feel as if the entire world is against us.

Much of our opposition comes through the very necessary experiences we label or interpret as adversity, trials, tribulations, and suffering. Some of these difficulties are actually planned and built into our mortal curriculum by a loving God to test and prove us, as well as to provide experiences that will develop the divine nature within us. Sometimes they come through the temptations and attacks of Satan and his helpers in their determination to destroy us. These we all face equally. Many of our difficulties, however, come from the random, accidental misfortunes that we all risk by living in this imperfect world, or as the result of cruel and unjust treatment by people who attempt to misuse or abuse us.

Whether we are blessed or harmed by the trials of mortality depends not on what happens to us or why it happened as much as it does on our response to it. Job's response to his undeserved sufferings is inspiring. "Though he slay me, yet will I trust him" (Job 13:15). Instead of driving himself crazy by trying to figure out *why* all those bad things were happening to him, instead of trying to blame God for allowing them, he said, "The Lord gave, and the Lord hath taken away; blessed be the name of the Lord" and "in all this Job sinned not, nor charged God foolishly" (Job 1:21–22). The difficulties we experience will be easier to endure (and profit from) when we regard them as divine homework assignments. "It is good for me that I have been afflicted; that I might learn thy statutes" (Psalm 119:71).

Staying happy and victorious in spite of what happens to us is achieved by appreciating the value of every mortal experience, whether it is enjoyable or not. Paul said, "We are troubled on every side, yet not distressed; we are perplexed, but not in despair" (2 Corinthians 4:8). This attitude of gratitude for mortality's learning experiences reminds us of President Gordon B. Hinckley, who said, "It isn't as bad as you sometimes think it is. It all works out. Don't worry. I say that to myself every morning. It will all work out. If you do your best, it will all work out. Put your trust in God, and move forward with faith and confidence in the future."[1]

"IF GOD BE FOR US, WHO CAN BE AGAINST US?"

The scriptures promise that no matter how unpleasant things may seem to our limited understanding, all mortal difficulties will *work together for our good* and *give us the experiences* that we need to become like Christ—if we *allow* them to. For example, "Ye cannot behold with your natural eyes, for the present time, the design of your God concerning those things which shall come hereafter, and the glory which shall follow after much tribulation" (D&C 58:3). "And we know that all things work together for good to them that love God, to them who are the called according to his purpose" (Romans 8:28; see also D&C 90:24; 98:3; 100:15; 105:40; 122:5–7).

But all things do not necessarily "work together for our good" or provide growing experiences to those who respond negatively or impatiently. We oftentimes forget that these unpleasant difficulties are not "against us" but are the very tutoring lessons of mortality that we fought a war for the privilege of coming here to experience. When we get all tangled up in the seeming injustices of our trials, blaming God or someone else for the very situations that allow us to learn and grow, we negate the benefits they were intended to provide and unwittingly prevent them from "working together for our good."

Ye fearful Saints, fresh courage take;
The clouds ye so much dread
Are big with mercy and shall break
In blessings on your head.[2]

When Jesus taught, "Resist not evil: but whosoever shall smite thee on thy right cheek, turn to him the other also" (Matthew 5:39), He was teaching a higher response to unpleasant and unwanted circumstances such as criticism, disrespectful or offensive treatment, even deliberate ridicule—mental and emotional slaps upon the cheek, if you will. It is in these unjustified offenses that we have a magnificent opportunity to rise above opposition and become more like Christ.

This principle of accepting our unwanted circumstances can also bring peace when we apply it to the broader difficulties we label as adversity and tribulation. Because of our need to learn by making choices and overcoming opposition, Jesus warned, "In the world ye shall have tribulation" (John 16:33), and Paul said "that we must through much tribulation enter into the kingdom of God" (Acts 14:22). Jesus promised blessings for enduring our difficulties without "resisting" the evil of such circumstances when He said, "He that is faithful in tribulation, the reward of the same is greater in the kingdom of heaven" (D&C 58:2).

"IF GOD BE FOR US, WHO CAN BE AGAINST US?"

Paul, who suffered greatly for his attempts to serve Christ, said, "I have learned, in whatsoever state I am, therewith to be content" (Philippians 4:11). We see his attitude reflected in the last words of Ether, the only righteous survivor of his entire culture: "Whether the Lord will that I be translated, or that I suffer the will of the Lord in the flesh, it mattereth not, if it so be that I am saved in the kingdom of God" (Ether 15:34). Moroni expressed the same thought at the end of his life (see Mormon 8:4). They both could have jeopardized their rewards by feeling resentful of being left alone without friends, family, or fellow believers. But they refused to resist the evil of their lonely circumstance, saying that they were content and that nothing else mattered to them as long as they proved faithful to the end.

"IF GOD BE FOR US, WHO CAN BE AGAINST US?"

Jesus warned of the most dangerous force "against us," the attacks from Satan, when He said, "Fear not them which kill the body, but are not able to kill the soul: but rather fear him which is able to destroy both soul and body in hell" (Matthew 10:28). In other words, the real dangers to our eternal destiny come not so much from the inconvenient adversities of mortality, but from the attacks of Satan. "For we wrestle not against flesh and blood," warned Paul, "but against principalities, against powers, against the rulers of the darkness of this world, against spiritual wickedness in high places" (Ephesians 6:12). For we know that "the devil is an enemy unto God, and fighteth against him continually, and inviteth and enticeth to sin, and to do that which is evil continually" (Moroni 7:12).

It appears that in his miserable existence, one of Satan's greatest pleasures is the victory he achieves when he persuades us to misuse our bodies or to break our covenants. "And thus he goeth up and down, to and fro in the earth, seeking to destroy the souls of men," for "he seeketh that all men might be miserable like unto himself" (D&C 10:27; 2 Nephi 2:27). Nevertheless, "though I walk through the valley of the shadow of death, I will fear no evil; for thou art with me . . . [and] . . . preparest a table before me in the presence of mine enemies" (Psalm 23:4–5).

Satan and his spirits have great power of persuasion and, if we will allow it, even possession, but there are boundaries beyond which they are not allowed to go. As Joseph Smith said, "The devil has no power over us only as we permit him."[3] ElRay L. Christiansen further emphasized, "Satan and his aides no doubt may know our inclinations, our carnal tastes and desires, but *they cannot compel a righteous person to do evil* if he seeks help from the Lord. Too many try to blame Satan when in reality the fault lies within themselves because they yield to his enticements."[4]

Satan tries to make us feel that we are alone in our battles with temptation, adversity, and other discouragements, but the Lord has said, "Be not afraid of [such circumstances]: for I am with thee to deliver thee, saith the Lord" (Jeremiah 1:8), and "your God is he that goeth with you, to fight for you against your enemies, to save you" (Deuteronomy 20:4).

Satan would also have us feel overwhelmed and outnumbered, but as Mary F. Foulger of the Relief Society general board advised, "Remember that you and the Lord constitute a majority."[5]

"IF GOD BE FOR US, WHO CAN BE AGAINST US?"

Because of His divine power to emanate His influence throughout the universe, Christ is "not far from every one of us," even though His physical presence may be elsewhere (Acts 17:27). "I the Lord am with you, and will stand by you," the Savior promised, and "I will go before your face. I will be on your right hand and on your left, and my Spirit will be in your hearts, and mine angels round about you, to bear you up" (D&C 68:6; 84:88). The words of an inspired hymn promise:

Fear not, I am with thee; oh, be not dismayed,
For I am thy God and will still give thee aid.
I'll strengthen thee, help thee, and cause thee to stand, . . .
Upheld by my righteous, omnipotent hand.[6]

"IF GOD BE FOR US, WHO CAN BE AGAINST US?"

Conclusion: How could applying the principles taught by this chapter's question help you to feel better about yourself, improve your relationship with the Lord, and lead you to greater feelings of happiness and peace?

NOTES

1. "Excerpts from Addresses of President Gordon B. Hinckley," *Ensign*, October 2000, 73.
2. "God Moves in a Mysterious Way," *Hymns*, 285.
3. *Teachings of the Prophet Joseph Smith*, 181.
4. ElRay L. Christiansen, "Questions and Answers," *New Era*, July 1975, 49; emphasis added.
5. "Motherhood and the Family," *Ensign*, November 1980, 105.
6. "How Firm a Foundation" *Hymns*, 85.

CHAPTER NINETEEN

IS ANY THING TOO HARD FOR THE LORD?

And they said unto him, Where is Sarah thy wife? And he said, Behold, in the tent.

And he said, I will certainly return unto thee according to the time of life; and, lo, Sarah thy wife shall have a son. And Sarah heard it in the tent door, which was behind him.

Now Abraham and Sarah were old and well stricken in age; and it ceased to be with Sarah after the manner of women.

Therefore Sarah laughed within herself, saying, After I am waxed old shall I have pleasure, my lord being old also?

And the Lord said unto Abraham, Wherefore did Sarah laugh, saying, Shall I of a surety bear a child, which am old?

Is any thing too hard for the Lord? At the time appointed I will return unto thee, according to the time of life, and Sarah shall have a son. (Genesis 18:9–14)

———

ALMOST THE LAST words Christ spoke before ascending into heaven, leaving His work in the hands of the apostles were, "All power is given unto me in heaven and in earth" (Matthew 28:18). All power! Unlimited power! Power to do the seemingly impossible! This possession of "all power" means "he hath all power unto the fulfilling of all his words" (1 Nephi 9:6), as well as unlimited power and resources with which to "supply all your need according to his riches in glory" (Philippians 4:19). In other words, "*There is nothing* that the Lord thy God shall take in his heart to do but what he will do it" (Abraham 3:17; emphasis added).

Of all the things Jesus could have said at the time of His departure, why did He choose to speak of His unlimited power? Perhaps it was because the Savior knew that we were going to encounter many difficult situations, both in building the kingdom and in perfecting our individual characters, that would surpass our limitations—situations that would be impossible to resolve without His help.

While Jesus was in Cana, a nobleman from Capernaum came to him pleading for the life of his son who was dying. Satisfied that the man was sincere and not merely seeking a sign, the Savior simply said, "Go thy way; thy son liveth" (John 4:46–53). It is not necessary for Christ to be physically present do His work. Perhaps that is why He twice emphasized that this unlimited power was given to Him both "in heaven *and* in earth" (Matthew 28:18; emphasis added), and also later affirmed to Joseph Smith, "And he received all power, *both in heaven* and *on earth*" (D&C 93:17; emphasis added).

"IS ANY THING TOO HARD FOR THE LORD?"

Our answer to this question depends on the focus of our attention and our faith. If our thoughts and fears are focused on the restricting limitations of our circumstances, which make it appear difficult, if not impossible, for God to do what we need, then our faith may be diminished and insufficient. If we focus on the scriptural and historical assurance that God Almighty is truly omnipotent, having unlimited power to do the seemingly impossible, then our faith can be sufficient to pull down the blessings we need.

It is not so difficult to have faith in Christ's power to help us when we can see several ways He could answer our prayers and fill our needs. But real faith is the faith that looks past the limitations of our seemingly impossible situations, the faith that confidently trusts Him even when we cannot imagine a solution or see any possible means of deliverance. Too often, instead of testifying, "there is nothing too hard for thee" (Jeremiah 32:17), we echo the same question as Nephi's doubtful brothers: "How is it possible?" (1 Nephi 3:31).

Laman and Lemuel did not want to go back to Jerusalem and face the difficulty of obtaining the brass plates from Laban. When the first attempt failed, they vented their anger on Nephi with angry words and beat him with a rod. They were so focused on the overwhelming difficulty of their assignment that even when an angel interrupted the beating and promised, "The Lord will deliver Laban into your hands," they still could not believe (1 Nephi 3:22–31).

"How is it possible," they whined, "that the Lord will deliver Laban into our hands?" And then, overwhelmed by the limitations of their options, they focused on the obvious mountain of difficulty: "Behold, he is a mighty man, and he can command fifty, yea, even he can slay fifty; then why not us?" (1 Nephi 3:31). Nephi's attention and faith was focused not on the *difficulties,* but on *God's power* to find a way around their difficulties. "Let us go up again unto Jerusalem, and let us be faithful in keeping the commandments of the Lord," he encouraged, "for behold *he is mightier than all the earth,* then why not mightier than Laban and his fifty, yea, or even than his tens of thousands?" (1 Nephi 4:1; emphasis added).

Elder Marvin J. Ashton taught, "Roadblocks to eternal progress are cast aside when resolves are made that no man needs to walk alone. It is a happy day when we come to know that with God's help nothing is impossible for us."[1] Thus, God's answers to our prayers are never restrained by the limitations of our seemingly impossible circumstances, "for there is no restraint to the Lord to save by many or by few" (1 Samuel 14:6). See Judges, chapter 7, for example, where the Lord reduced an Israelite army from 32,000 men to only 300 soldiers to demonstrate this very point.

There is *no situation* we can encounter from which Christ cannot deliver us, whether it is physical, mental, emotional, or spiritual. Indeed, "he is able also to save them *to the uttermost* that come unto God by him," and "*he has all power* to save every man that believeth on his name and bringeth forth fruit meet for repentance" (Hebrews 7:25; Alma 12:15; also Philippians 3:21; emphasis added).

"IS ANY THING TOO HARD FOR THE LORD?"

One reason we can have complete trust in the Lord's power is that all the elements of this world are in total and ready obedience to His every command (see Helaman 12:7–17). Whenever it suits His purpose, He who created the earth has unlimited power to modify the way we see and experience the elements.

For example, Pharaoh responded to Moses by defiantly challenging,

"Who is the Lord, that I should obey his voice to let Israel go?" (Exodus 5:2). Jehovah, the premortal Christ, responded through Moses by demonstrating His power over the elements as He taught Pharaoh and all the world that the things that are impossible with men are possible with God (Luke 18:27; also Matthew 19:26; Mark 10:27).

Among other things, He changed the water of the Nile River into blood, as well as all the water in all the containers in the entire land (see Exodus 7:19–21). He then transformed the dusty sands of Egypt into living lice that infected man and beast alike (see Exodus 8:16–17). How could He bring life out of dust? "With men it is impossible, but not with God: for with God all things are possible" (Mark 10:27). The God of the impossible is not limited to the method of procreation He requires us to use. To the Jews, who boasted of their alleged superiority because Abraham was their ancestor, Christ declared, "I say unto you, That God is able of these stones to raise up children unto Abraham" (Luke 3:8).

"IS ANY THING TOO HARD FOR THE LORD?"

When Jehovah led Israel out of Egypt, their destination was Mount Sinai. He could have easily circumvented the Red Sea by directing them to pass above the headwaters, so why did He allow the Israelites to be trapped between the Red Sea and Pharaoh with his army of horsemen and over 600 chariots? Perhaps He led them into this situation from which there was no possible escape, no solution conceivable to the mortal mind, because He was prepared to do the unimaginable; to demonstrate that He truly does have all power in heaven and on earth.

To the fearful, faithless Israelites, Moses said, "Fear ye not, stand still, and see the salvation of the Lord, which he will shew to you today. . . . And Moses stretched out his hand over the sea; and the Lord caused the sea to go back by a strong east wind. . . . And the children of Israel went into the midst of the sea upon the dry ground: and the waters were a wall unto them on their right hand, and on their left" (Exodus 14:13, 21–22). Perhaps Jehovah parted the Red Sea to demonstrate that "with God *nothing shall be impossible*" (Luke 1:37; emphasis added) and to help us learn that we can depend upon Him in any problem or need, no matter how hopeless the circumstances appear in our limited vision. As the brother of Jared testified, "And I know, O Lord, that thou hast all power, and *can do whatsoever thou wilt for the benefit of man"* (Ether 3:4; emphasis added).

Later He would send an unexpected and unprecedented storm in which hailstones fell from the skies to destroy an army that would otherwise have defeated God's people (see Joshua 10:1–11). On another occasion the Israelites were saved by nothing more than a disturbing "noise" from the Lord that filled the enemy army with fear and turned them back from the attack (see 2 Kings 7:1–7). To free Alma's people from a bondage they had no way to escape, the Lord gave them time to flee to safety by simply causing a deep sleep to come upon the enemy (see Mosiah 24:19). David was similarly protected in 1 Samuel 26:12.

"IS ANY THING TOO HARD FOR THE LORD?"

As the Israelites wandered through the wilderness, they grew tired of having nothing to eat but manna, and complained. The Lord was displeased with their murmuring and lack of gratitude. He told Moses He would provide them with so much flesh to eat that it would become loathsome to them. Moses reminded the Lord that there were hundreds of thousands of people and doubted there would be enough meat to go around even if they killed every animal in their camp (see Numbers 11:1–21). This was to be a learning experience for Moses as well as Israel. "And the Lord said to Moses, *Is the Lord's hand waxed short?* thou shalt see now whether my word shall come to pass unto thee or not" (Numbers 11:23; emphasis added).

The miracle that soon followed was stunning: "And there went forth a wind from the Lord, and brought quails from the sea, and let them fall by the camp, as it were a day's journey on this side, and as it were a day's journey on the other side, round about the camp, and as it were two cubits high upon the face of the earth" (Numbers 11:31).

We know the Lord also used a special wind to accomplish the impossible task of propelling the ships of the Nephites and Jaredites across the ocean to the American continent without engines (see Ether 6:5).

"IS ANY THING TOO HARD FOR THE LORD?"

When we find ourselves in doubt of our own limited abilities, we should turn to the Savior, who not only has all power but also has promised, "My grace is sufficient for all men" (Ether 12:27). We know that He magnified a few loaves of bread and fishes to feed thousands (see Mark 6). Why then, is it so hard to believe that He can magnify our efforts until we gain victory over our stumbling blocks? We also know that He changed ordinary water into wine (see John 2). Why is it so hard to believe that He can transform ordinary men and women into His divine image? To believe that we cannot overcome our problems and inappropriate behaviors is to deny Christ's power. "Yea, and how is it that ye have forgotten that *the Lord is able to do all things according to his will,* for the children of men, if it so be that they exercise faith in him? Wherefore, let us be faithful to him" (1 Nephi 7:12; emphasis added).

"Is any thing too hard for the Lord?"

Conclusion: How could applying the principles taught by this chapter's question help you to feel better about yourself, improve your relationship with the Lord, and lead you to greater feelings of happiness and peace?

Notes

1. Marvin J. Ashton, "Roadblocks to Progress," *Ensign*, May 1979, 69.

CHAPTER TWENTY

LORD, HOW OFT SHALL MY BROTHER SIN AGAINST ME, AND I FORGIVE HIM?

Then came Peter to him, and said, Lord, how oft shall my brother sin against me, and I forgive him? till seven times?

Jesus saith unto him, I say not unto thee, Until seven times: but, Until seventy times seven. (Matthew 18:21–22)

A KIND AND forgiving Savior has promised, "As often as my people repent will I forgive them their trespasses against me" (Mosiah 26:30). Not only does He eagerly *forgive* every repentant person, but He actually *welcomes* them to His fellowship, promising that when we seek to draw near to him, He will respond by drawing near to us (see D&C 88:63).

But he has conditioned this welcome fellowship upon the prerequisite that we must first cleanse our hearts and relationships of all feelings of bitterness and resentment by forgiving those who have hurt or offended us. He defined this prerequisite when He said, "I, the Lord, will forgive whom I will forgive, but of you it is required to forgive all men" (D&C 64:10) and "he that forgiveth not his neighbor's trespasses when he says that he repents, the same hath brought himself under condemnation" (Mosiah 26:31). As H. Burke Peterson of the Presiding Bishopric said, "No one can be classed as a true follower of the Savior who is not in the process of removing from his heart and mind every feeling of ill will, bitterness, hatred, envy, or jealousy toward another."[1]

It is one thing to forgive someone an occasional offense, but this business of forgiving repeat offenders "seventy times seven" is altogether another matter. Now we are talking about really stretching to become like Christ, especially considering that the higher the number of repeating offenses, the less likely the offender will show any remorse or repentance. So let's go right to the issue of what the Lord requires of us in response to a cruel person who refuses to change or stop hurting us.

Taking it to the extreme test, what if this person says, "I'm glad I hurt you and I'll probably do it again." What then? The answer is unchanged, even toward those who are cruel and unrepentant: "I, the Lord, will forgive whom I will forgive, but of you it is required to forgive *all* men" (D&C 64:10; emphasis added). The scriptures contain no exclusion clause based on who is right or who is wrong; they only say that we must *always* forgive, whether the other party is repentant or not (see D&C 98:39–43). Even until "seventy times seven."

There is no other way to be right with our Savior than to freely forgive, without regard to another's repentance or lack of it. It is the condition of our hearts that the Lord had in mind when He counseled the seventy-times-seven forgiveness. But this does *not* mean we have to leave ourselves vulnerable to repeated acts of aggression. If we are in an abusive situation, we should seek safety and protection from those who would deliberately harm us.

Sometimes we think we are doing others a favor when we forgive them. But we are mostly helping ourselves, because when we hate someone or hold bitter feelings and grudges toward them, we are really hurting ourselves more than them. Let's consider a couple of reasons for this.

First of all, whatever we hold in our focus of attention holds us. So refusing to forgive an injustice fills our souls with spiritual poison and chains us to the pains of the past. It keeps past wounds from healing and prevents us from moving forward toward the Lord because our unforgiving disobedience has driven the Spirit from our own lives (see Mosiah 2:36). Elder Peterson also counseled, "The longer the poison of resentment and unforgiveness stays in a body, the greater and longer lasting is its destructive effect. As long as we blame others for our condition or circumstance and build a wall of self-justification around ourselves, our strength will diminish and our power and ability to rise above our situation will fade away. The poison of revenge, or of unforgiving thoughts or attitudes, unless removed, will destroy the soul in which it is harbored."[2]

We all hold the key to removing those self-inflicted chains with an act of forgiveness, but unfortunately, some of us would rather cling to the wounds to justify our bitter feelings. If we don't release that spiritual poison with an act of total forgiveness, it will rot and fester inside us, increasing our misery. It is a self-imposed sentence of unnecessary suffering. As Karen Burton Mains explained, "When our grievance grows to hatred, we become slaves of the very persons we hate. We are bound to them with chains that leave us no peace. Waking, we are haunted by their presence. Our sleeping is shadowed by their deeds. Our memories are clouded by their wrongdoing. Their present actions grind and gore us. We have allowed hatred to become our incarceration."[3]

Second, the Savior can overlook many imperfections in those who draw near to Him, but refusing to forgive erects almost impenetrable barriers between the Lord and us. Attempting to judge another person and withholding our forgiveness from them denies *ourselves* of the very same blessing from the Lord, for "if ye do not forgive, neither will your Father which is in heaven forgive your trespasses" (Mark 11:26). Who can afford such a high penalty? Refusing to forgive shows that we are more interested in having someone to blame than we are in letting go of the hurt and becoming closer to the Savior. It also allows us to set ourselves up in the Savior's place as that person's judge, as if we know better than God when (or whether) that offender should be forgiven. What an offense it is to a magnificent, forgiving Savior when we insist on clinging to past injuries and condemning people instead of surrendering that pain to Christ as He has commanded.

The Savior warned, "Judge not that ye be not judged. For with what judgment ye judge, ye shall be judged: and with what measure ye mete, it shall be measured to you again" (Matthew 7:1–2). What an offense to a magnificent, forgiving Savior when we insist on clinging to past injuries and condemning people instead of surrendering that pain to Christ as He has commanded.

Forgiving the offender does not mean we are condoning the sin. By forgiving we are not agreeing with the wrong this person has done. We are only showing that the person who hurt us is more important than the mistake they made and that being right with the Savior is more important to us than making someone pay for what they did to us. As Elder Theodore M. Burton said, "We need not be tolerant of sin, but we must become tolerant and forgiving of the sinner. . . . It is wicked to reject a child of God simply because he made an error."[4]

Speaking of how we should deal with those who continue to hurt us or refuse to repent of past offenses, the Lord said, "Ye ought to say in your hearts—let God judge between me and thee, and reward thee according to thy deeds" (D&C 64:11). That may sound like a curse, but it is not. It is but another way of giving the burden to the Lord—of acknowledging His right to be the judge. He has commanded, "Leave judgment alone with me, for it is mine and I will repay" (D&C 82:23). There is great healing when we let go of the pain and refuse to punish the offender, when we surrender the injustice to Him who suffered the greatest injustice of all. Leaving the judgment of the offender to the Lord is the path to freedom and peace, even though the offense may never be made right in this life.

Forgiving those who hurt us deeply and repeatedly is one of the most difficult things the Lord has asked us to do. And sooner or later, every person will be tested by a personal injury or injustice so painful that it will seem impossible to feel forgiving. Sometimes our wounds go so deep that letting go of the pain may actually be beyond our mortal ability. But the Lord has provided a way out of this problem.

Contrary to what one might think, the ability to forgive is not dependent on a thick skin or strong will power, and it seldom depends on our emotions. We cannot turn our feelings on or off like a faucet, and the Lord doesn't expect us to. In His role as our Savior, Jesus Christ will enable us to do what we are willing to do but cannot accomplish by ourselves. Forgiveness begins with a *decision*—a mental decision to turn the pain over to the Lord and to accept His help in accomplishing what He has commanded us to do.

No matter how deep the wound or how great the pain, we can always decide to be *willing* to forgive, at least *mentally willing* to let go; *willing* to bear the injustice without complaining about it, and that is the starting point that allows Christ to rescue us. When we offer that sacrifice of obedience to His command to forgive all men, even until "seventy times seven," Christ will reward that *willingness* by healing our emotional wounds and removing the feelings that blocked our forgiving, and He will also reward us with overflowing feelings of peace and comfort, even with love for the one who wronged us.

A woman who wrote about her experience illustrates this divine rescue from feelings that we cannot release by ourselves but which we are willing to place on the altar of sacrifice. All her life she had been possessed by feelings of resentment toward a relative who had abused her as a child, leaving her with a permanent, painful physical condition. She often wondered at the injustice of the suffering the abuse had caused and why she had to continue suffering, even as an adult. One day, as she listened to a talk in church, her heart was touched. The Spirit bore witness to her that she should forgive the man who had wronged her and that *she could do so with the help of the Lord Jesus Christ.* When she finally surrendered this terrible injustice to the Savior, she was at last set free. She said, "The price for that sin has already been paid by Him in Gethsemane. I have no right to hold on to it and demand justice, so I gladly hand it back to Him and rejoice in His love and mercy. My heart is so full of joy, peace, and gratitude and love! Words cannot express my feelings."[5]

"LORD, HOW OFT SHALL MY BROTHER SIN AGAINST ME, AND I FORGIVE HIM?"

Conclusion: How could applying the principles taught by this chapter's question help you to feel better about yourself, improve your relationship with the Lord, and lead you to greater feelings of happiness and peace?

NOTES

1. "Removing the Poison of an Unforgiving Spirit," *Ensign*, November 1983, 60.
2. "Removing the Poison of an Unforgiving Spirit," *Ensign*, November 1983, 59.
3. Karen Burton Mains, *The Key to a Loving Heart* (Carmel, New York: Guidepost Books, 1979), 78.
4. "To Forgive Is Divine," *Ensign*, May 1983, 71.
5. Personal correspondence.

CHAPTER TWENTY-ONE

WHY AM I ANGRY BECAUSE OF MINE ENEMY?

O then, if I have seen so great things, if the Lord in his condescension unto the children of men hath visited men in so much mercy, why should my heart weep and my soul linger in the valley of sorrow, and my flesh waste away, and my strength slacken, because of mine afflictions?

And why should I yield to sin, because of my flesh? Yea, why should I give way to temptations, that the evil one have place in my heart to destroy my peace and afflict my soul? Why am I angry because of mine enemy?

Awake, my soul! No longer droop in sin. Rejoice, O my heart, and give place no more for the enemy of my soul.

Do not anger again because of mine enemies. Do not slacken my strength because of mine afflictions. (2 Nephi 4:26–29)

———————

SOMEONE HAS SAID that one of the heaviest loads a man can carry is a grudge, and the Chinese philosopher Confucius said, "To be wronged is nothing unless you continue to remember it."[1] Scripture counsels, "Let all bitterness, and wrath, and anger, and clamour, and evil speaking, be put away from you, with all malice" (Ephesians 4:31). And also, "Thou shalt not avenge, nor bear any grudge against the children of thy people, but thou shalt love thy neighbour as thyself" (Leviticus 19:18).

When we feel angry because someone has injured or offended us, it is because we are more concerned about their affect on us than we are about how we might love and help them to do better. Spencer W. Kimball emphasized that "the spirit of revenge, of retaliation, of bearing a grudge is entirely foreign to the gospel of the gentle, forgiving Jesus Christ."[2] Responding to an offense or injury with anger allows those unkind acts to plunge us into feelings of self-pity and resentment. If unchecked, such feelings can quickly expand into hostility, rage, fury, wrath, and indignation. "Rejoice, O my heart, and *give place no more* for the enemy of my soul" (2 Nephi 4:28; emphasis added).

"WHY AM I ANGRY BECAUSE OF MINE ENEMY?"

What is interesting is that harboring anger and refusing to forgive someone always hurts us more than it hurts the other person. Perhaps the Lord was warning of this when He said, "Whosoever is angry with his brother shall be in danger of his judgment" and "whosoever shall say Thou fool [criticizing and complaining of unjust treatment], shall be in danger of hell fire" (3 Nephi 12:22). When we choose to look *inward* and focus on our injury, rather than looking *outward* to see how we might help the offender, the first and most immediate penalty for indulging anger is the loss of spirituality and receptivity to the Holy Spirit. Then, like an infection, it fills our souls with a spiritual poison that keeps our emotional wounds from healing. If we don't cleanse that wound with an act of forgiveness, the anger and grudge will rot and fester inside us until we are miserable and we probably won't even understand why.

As Spencer W. Kimball said, "Bitterness has a way of poisoning the mind and killing the spirit. One should take no chances of permitting such situations to become sore and gangrenous, for who can tell when one might slip across the line?"[3]

"WHY AM I ANGRY BECAUSE OF MINE ENEMY?"

Feeling anger and wanting to retaliate in kind is a normal, human, natural-man response. However, trying to hurt someone for hurting us prevents our having peace, kindness, and tolerance in our hearts. Yes, the price of forgiveness is high, but the rewards are more than worth it. As Ruby Spilsbury Brown, a grieved mother, said, "Before the Lord [can] put comfort into our torn hearts, we must get hatred and bitterness out of our hearts."[4] Thus, Christ has asked us to rise above the natural-man feelings and to respond as He did. "*Love* your enemies," He said, "*bless* them that curse you, *do good* to them that hate you, and *pray* for them who despitefully use you and persecute you" (3 Nephi 12:44; emphasis added; Matthew 5:44; Luke 6:27–28).

He also said that we should *"rejoice, and be exceeding glad"* when "men shall revile you, and persecute you, and shall say all manner of evil against you falsely, for my sake" (Matthew 5:11–12; emphasis added). One reason to rejoice instead of becoming angry is that it provides us with a magnificent opportunity to rise above the opposition and become more like Christ. "To retaliate and fight back is human," said Spencer W. Kimball, "but to accept indignities as did the Lord is divine."[5]

Sometimes the spirit of forgiveness is carried to the loftiest height—to rendering assistance to the offender. Not to be revengeful, not to seek what outraged justice might demand, to leave the offender in God's hands—this is admirable. But to return good for evil, this is the sublime expression of Christian love.[6]

There is great power and peace in predetermining our emotional position in life without letting our feelings depend upon what others do. One way to accomplish this is to use the admonition the Lord gave us when He said, "Ye ought to say in your hearts—let God judge between me and thee, and reward thee according to thy deeds" (D&C 64:11). That may sound like a curse, but it is not. "Fear not thine enemies," He said, "for they are in mine hands and I will do my pleasure with them" (D&C 136:30). There is great healing when we refuse to judge or punish the offender, when we surrender the injustice to Him who suffered the greatest injustices of all. Leaving the judgment of the offender to the Lord is the path to freedom and peace, even though the offense may never be righted in this life.

"WHY AM I ANGRY BECAUSE OF MINE ENEMY?"

But what can we do in situations where our pain is so great that we are not only unwilling to forgive, but are consumed with anger and a desire for revenge? Even then there is hope if we will humble ourselves by laying that anger and hate on the altar of sacrifice, as we offer a prayer of surrender and *willingness* to be helped. For example, we stand in awe at the faithfulness of Nephi. His family murmured because of their sufferings and turned on him in bitter persecution and ridicule, even seeking his life. "Nevertheless," he said, "I did look unto my God, and I did praise him all the day long, and I did not murmur against the Lord because of mine afflictions" (1 Nephi 18:16). But even he had to pray for help to deal with his very natural feelings of pain. "Behold," he said, "it came to pass that I, Nephi, did cry much unto the Lord my God, because of the anger of my brethren" (2 Nephi 5:1).

When we are hurting and feeling anger, we might pray in this manner: "Father, there is no way I can overcome these feelings by myself. In fact, to be honest, I don't even want to forgive this person. But I know this attitude is wrong. I know holding on to anger and refusing to forgive is harmful, both to the other person involved and to myself. So, Heavenly Father, I am asking thee to help me surrender my bitterness. *I am asking thee to make me willing to be willing.*"

"WHY AM I ANGRY BECAUSE OF MINE ENEMY?"

A scriptural warning that can help motivate us to pray such a prayer and to sincerely lay our wounds on the altar of sacrifice says, "If ye forgive men their trespasses, your heavenly Father will also forgive you: But if ye forgive not men their trespasses, neither will your Father forgive your trespasses" (Matthew 6:14). As Sherrie Johnson emphasized, "Only by forgiving and forgetting—letting go of our bitterness and hurt—do we free ourselves to progress." She also encouraged, "Change of any kind is difficult, but forgiving and forgetting is perhaps the hardest kind of change. This change is beyond yourself, but is attainable when you seek and accept the help of Heavenly Father. He can give you the strength you lack."[7]

"WHY AM I ANGRY BECAUSE OF MINE ENEMY?"

Conclusion: How could applying the principles taught by this chapter's question help you to feel better about yourself, improve your relationship with the Lord, and lead you to greater feelings of happiness and peace?

NOTES

1. As quoted by Spencer W. Kimball, *The Miracle of Forgiveness*, 266, 299.
2. *The Miracle of Forgiveness*, 265.
3. *The Miracle of Forgiveness*, 121–22.
4. As quoted by Spencer W. Kimball, *The Miracle of Forgiveness*, 289
5. *The Miracle of Forgiveness*, 113.
6. Spencer W. Kimball, *The Miracle of Forgiveness*, 284.
7. "A Difficult Kind of Forgiving," *Ensign*, January 1985, 60.

CHAPTER TWENTY-TWO

BELIEVE YE THAT I AM ABLE TO DO THIS?

And when Jesus departed thence, two blind men followed him, crying, and saying, Thou Son of David, have mercy on us.

And when he was come into the house, the blind men came to him: and Jesus saith unto them, Believe ye that I am able to do this? They said unto him, Yea, Lord.

Then touched he their eyes, saying, According to your faith be it unto you. (Matthew 9:27–29)

THE TWO KEY words in this question are *believe* and *able*. They are the same keys that determine how much faith we have for our own prayer requests. We note the question was not if they believed that Christ *would* give them sight, but whether they believed He *had the power* to do so. That is a much narrower question, a question that can only be answered yes or no. And it is the starting point of faith, because if we cannot even focus on His unlimited power to do or accomplish whatever it is that we need from him, how could we ever move toward the faith that He *will* do it?

Two of scripture's dominant themes are the assurance that God is not only *able* to do the seemingly impossible for us, but also His eager *willingness* and *desire* to show His love by giving us blessings. Throughout the centuries, our Savior and Heavenly Father have demonstrated that they are Gods of miracles and seemingly impossible circumstances. "For with God nothing shall be impossible" (Luke 1:37) and "there is nothing that the Lord thy God shall take in his heart to do but what he will do it" (Abraham 3:17). The Lord said, "I will show unto the children of men that *I am able* to do mine own work" (2 Nephi 27:21; emphasis added), and Paul testified that God's unlimited power "is able to do *exceeding abundantly* above all that we ask or think" (Ephesians 3:20; emphasis added).

"BELIEVE YE THAT I AM ABLE TO DO THIS?"

As to His *willingness* to bless us, the scriptures teach that God is not only "mindful of every people, whatsoever land [or circumstance] they may be in," but that "his bowels of mercy are over all the earth" (Alma 26:37) and that "he doeth not anything save it be for the benefit of the world; for he loveth the world" (2 Nephi 26:24). Not only do the scriptures emphasize that "no good thing will he withhold from them that walk uprightly" (Psalm 84:11), but also that it "pleases" God to bless us with the good things of life (see D&C 59:16–20). He said, "I, the Lord . . . delight to honor those who serve me in righteousness and in truth unto the end" (D&C 76:5).

The Lord's eagerness to use His power on our behalf is illustrated by a leper who came "beseeching him, and kneeling down to him, and saying unto him, *If thou wilt*, thou canst make me clean. And Jesus, moved with compassion, put forth his hand, and touched him, and saith unto him, *I will*; be thou clean" (Mark 1:40–41; emphasis added). Not only is God *willing* to grant us blessings, He has actually promised, "I will *order* all things for your good, as fast as ye are able to receive them" (D&C 111:11; emphasis added).

The Savior's reply to the two blind men is one that often discourages us, *"According to your faith* be it unto you" (Matthew 9:29; emphasis added). Moroni's challenge also puts the responsibility for miracles and blessings upon our faith: "If the day cometh that the power and gifts of God shall be done away among you, *it shall be because of unbelief"* (Moroni 10:24; emphasis added).

"BELIEVE YE THAT I AM ABLE TO DO THIS?"

One way to overcome this discouraging "my-faith-is-too-weak" hurdle is by realizing that receiving the divine intervention we need is not as dependent on *how much* faith we have as on *where we focus* the faith that we do have. If the overwhelming circumstances of your present defeat make the blessing you seek seem impossible, try placing your faith in the Savior's power and eagerness to bless you instead.

Another way to increase our faith is by using the word *expectation* in place of *belief.* The dictionary says that to "expect" something is to antici-pate it, to hope or await the probable occurrence of something that you consider reasonable. So to *believe* is simply to *expect. Un*belief or doubt simply means expecting no results.

Do you believe it would be possible to rehabilitate every prisoner in America so completely that we could eliminate every jail and prison within the next thirty years? You probably find your mind is immediately thinking of all the reasons this would be impossible. That's the way our minds have been trained to think—to limit our expectations. And if we can't even expect something to happen, how much chance is there that it ever will?

The scriptures refer to people who are perishing because of their "veil of unbelief" (see Alma 19:6; Ether 4:14–15). A veil of unbelief is like a mental or emotional blindfold that blocks all positive expectations and therefore, the flow of blessings. Unbelief not only darkens our minds, but is also considered a sin (see D&C 84:54; 58:15). If we never expect Christ to change us, how could He (see 3 Nephi 19:35)? When Jesus returned to Nazareth, He could have bestowed many blessings on His former friends and relatives, but they scorned Him and therefore, "he did not many mighty works there because of their unbelief" (Matthew 13:58). I wonder what "mighty works" He has been wanting to do in our lives but can't— because we won't let Him.

"BELIEVE YE THAT I AM ABLE TO DO THIS?"

While many blessings, miracles, and answers to prayer are dependent on our faith, the Lord does not require us to have superhuman or perfect belief and faith. In fact, He is so eager to help us rise above our doubts that if we feel that we lack sufficient faith to receive a needed healing or blessing, we can ask for our faith, trust, and expectation to be increased! A grieving father (with limited faith) who brought his son to Christ for healing illustrates this principle (see Mark 9:17–27).

For many years the boy had been tortured and almost killed by the demon that possessed his body. The most frequent symptoms of the possession were violent gnashing of the boy's teeth as he thrashed about on the ground in convulsions, foaming at the mouth. But the evil spirit also tried to kill the boy as it drove him into the fires to burn his body, or cast him into the water to drown him. We can scarcely imagine the family's emotional pain of having the boy suffer like that year after year with no medical help or hope of ever changing the situation, never daring to leave him unattended for even a moment. Surely it would have been difficult for that weary father to hope, difficult to believe, difficult to expect any change. "If thou canst do any thing," he said, "have compassion on us, and help us" (Mark 9:22).

In contrast, when the brother of Jared approached the Lord with the unprecedented request to make sixteen stones shine, so they might have light in their vessels and not have to cross the ocean in darkness, he said, with almost perfect faith, "I know, O Lord, that thou hast all power, and can do whatsoever thou wilt for the benefit of man" (Ether 3:4). But the boy's father came to Christ with a more normal weakness of faith: "If thou canst do anything, have compassion on us, and help us."

"BELIEVE YE THAT I AM ABLE TO DO THIS?"

Christ responded to his request by saying, "If thou canst believe, all things are possible to him that believeth" (Mark 9:23). This answer struck fear into the father and he began to cry. As the tears coursed down his face, in one last desperate attempt to help his son, he spoke for all of us who struggle with wavering faith, saying, "Lord, I believe; help thou mine *unbelief*" (Mark 9:24; emphasis added). In effect the father was saying, "Of course I believe. That's why I came to you for help. That's why I pray, but when things don't happen like I expect, or as quickly as I expect, I waver. I wonder—is it because of *me*, or is it a limitation of the *principles*? I *want* to believe. Please help me over my doubts. Help me to see this happening. Help me to anticipate its fulfillment. Give me hope. Help thou mine *expectations*."

But why was he crying when the Lord had just offered to help?

The father came for healing but discovered that Christ was not a magician whose favor one had to win, but a God of unlimited power whose blessings can only be limited by our own unbelief and lack of expectation.

He was crying because the burden had been tossed back to him and this made him afraid. He was surprised by the Lord's response. He had assumed everything was up to the Lord's power, but Christ had basically said, "Sure, I can to this. But it is more up to *you* and *your* belief than it is to my power." The man was crying in fear because he knew how weak his faith was.

How encouraging that his plea, "Help thou mine unbelief," did not anger the Lord or prevent the healing. It expressed his willingness, and that was enough. Christ commanded the evil spirit to give up the illegal habitation of the boy's body. Not only did Jesus say, "Come out of him," but also, "enter no more into him." It was to be a permanent healing.

"BELIEVE YE THAT I AM ABLE TO DO THIS?"

The Lord promised Abraham and Sarah a son of destiny when they were old and wrinkled, far past the age for bearing children. Abraham's unquestioning belief in the impossible promise is often cited as an example of faith toward which we should strive.

> And being not weak in faith, he considered not his own body now dead, when he was about an hundred years old, neither yet the deadness of Sara's womb:
>
> He staggered not at the promise of God through unbelief; but was strong in faith, giving glory to God;
>
> And being *fully persuaded* that, what he had promised, he was able also to perform. (Romans 4:19–21; emphasis added)

It would be wonderful to be "fully persuaded" in all things we need and request, wonderful to have the faith of Abraham or the brother of Jared. But until we reach that point, we are still allowed access to the blessings we need as long as we are humble enough to place our lesser, beginning faith in the Lord, asking, "Help thou mine unbelief."

"BELIEVE YE THAT I AM ABLE TO DO THIS?"

Conclusion: How could applying the principles taught by this chapter's question help you to feel better about yourself, improve your relationship with the Lord, and lead you to greater feelings of happiness and peace?

CHAPTER TWENTY-THREE

CAN A MAN TAKE FIRE IN HIS BOSOM, AND HIS CLOTHES NOT BE BURNED?

> Can a man take fire in his bosom, and his clothes not be burned?
>
> Can one go upon hot coals, and his feet not be burned?
>
> So he that goeth in to his neighbour's wife; whosoever toucheth her shall not be innocent. . . .
>
> But whoso committeth adultery with a woman lacketh understanding: he that doeth it destroyeth his own soul.
>
> A wound and dishonour shall he get; and his reproach shall not be wiped away. (Proverbs 6:27–29, 32–33)

THE FIRES AND coals referred to here are symbols of the power and danger of harmful lusts and passions indulged outside the bounds of marriage. The obvious answer to the questions is, no. We cannot play with the fires of illegitimate passion without being burned any more than we can avoid the consequences of placing our hand on a hot stove.

Every mortal choice and action has consequences, and no matter how cleverly we may think we can hide the secret sins of lustful indulgence, they are recorded in the book of life from which we will be judged, as well as within the very fibers of our minds and cellular structure as patterns of thought, habits and cravings. "There is nothing secret which is save it shall be revealed; there is no work of darkness save it shall be made manifest in the light" (2 Nephi 30:17).

"CAN A MAN TAKE FIRE IN HIS BOSOM, AND HIS CLOTHES NOT BE BURNED?"

In the premortal world we lived a long time as spirits, without physical bodies of flesh. Now we live in bodies that are strange and unfamiliar, fallen, natural-man bodies that are filled with sexual passions and that make us want things that are harmful and will hinder our progress. As Peter warned, "Dearly beloved, I beseech you as strangers and pilgrims [meaning new to this physical world], abstain from fleshly lusts, *which war against the soul*" (1 Peter 2:11; emphasis added).

Sexuality is a divine and beautiful gift from God. The Lord has asked us to reverence these sacred feelings and to reserve them exclusively for our legal and lawful marriage partner. As Spencer W. Kimball emphasized, "The law of chastity requires total abstinence *before* marriage and full fidelity *afterward*. It is the same for men and women."[1] In his determination to destroy us, Satan is continually enticing people to defile the sexual part of their nature through experimentation and indulgence outside of marriage.

"CAN A MAN TAKE FIRE IN HIS BOSOM, AND HIS CLOTHES NOT BE BURNED?"

Satan already failed to win us to his side in the premortal world, so now, in this physical world, his strategy is to capture us through the desires and vulnerabilities of our flesh. This strategy for using our bodies to defeat us is based on the immediacy of physical pleasures, and sexual transgressions have proven to be one of the easiest ways for him to accomplish that goal. "From whence come [these] wars and fightings among you? come they not hence, even of your lusts that war in your members [meaning parts of our bodies]?" (James 4:1).

There are probably more spiritual casualties and hearts broken in the combat zone of sexual sin than on any other battleground in Satan's war for our souls. As Melvin J. Ballard warned, "The most favorite method the enemy of our souls has employed in ages past and that he will employ today is to capture souls by leading them gently, step by step, towards the greatest and most destructive sin against spiritual life—immorality, the ultimate end of self-indulgence."[2]

"CAN A MAN TAKE FIRE IN HIS BOSOM, AND HIS CLOTHES NOT BE BURNED?"

Part of Christ's mission is to purify and sanctify our temple-bodies so they are worthy of His Spirit and companionship at all times. Satan's goal is to have us misuse and defile our bodies in ways that will prevent us from having the Lord's Spirit with us. Because Satan focuses so much of his effort on immorality, it is likely that every person living in this generation will have to face the challenge of overcoming sexual temptation, of choosing between virtue and lust.

Unbridled desires and passions lead us into the captivity of selfishness, which destroys our ability to love others, to feel concern, or to give service to others, because of preoccupation with our own pleasures. As Billy Graham warned, "The Bible makes plain that evil, when related to sex means not the use of something inherently corrupt but the *misuse* of something pure and good. It teaches clearly that sex can be a wonderful servant, but *a terrible master*: that it can be a creative force more powerful than any other in the fostering of a love, companionship, happiness or *can be the most destructive of all of life's forces*."[3]

Christ has challenged, *"Entangle not yourselves in sin,* but let your hands be clean" (D&C 88:86; emphasis added). Entangling ourselves in the web of sin refers to enslaving habits and addictions, but it can also refer to the foolishness of trying to juggle hot coals without being burned. Thinking we can indulge unworthy passions without suffering the consequences is one of Satan's most effective "it mattereth not" deceptions. It is something like throwing gasoline on a fire you are trying to extinguish. We cannot choose sin and escape becoming entangled in a web of captivity, especially when it comes to immorality, for "the wicked is snared in the work of his own hands," and "his mischief shall return upon his own head" (Psalms 9:16; 7:16).

"CAN A MAN TAKE FIRE IN HIS BOSOM, AND HIS CLOTHES NOT BE BURNED?"

Because of the law of accumulation, each choice we make for the way we use our time and our bodies either leads us *upward* toward greater spirituality, freedom, and self-mastery, or *downward* toward enslavement and sorrow. "Be not deceived; God is not mocked: for whatsoever a man soweth, that shall he also reap. For he that soweth to his flesh shall of the flesh reap corruption; but he that soweth to the Spirit shall of the Spirit reap life everlasting" (Galatians 6:7–8).

No one expects their initial compromising indulgence to lead to enslaving habits or addictions, but inasmuch as we always reap as we sow, there is no thought or choice that is too small to have a lasting effect. "His own iniquities shall take the wicked himself, and he shall be holden with the cords of his sins" (Proverbs 5:22). Everything we do with (or to) our physical bodies contributes to thought and habit patterns that can last into eternity, "for that same spirit which doth possess your bodies at the time that ye go out of this life, that same spirit will have power to possess your body in that eternal world" (Alma 34:34).

"CAN A MAN TAKE FIRE IN HIS BOSOM, AND HIS CLOTHES NOT BE BURNED?"

When the Bible says, "As he thinketh in his heart, so is he" (Proverbs 23:7), it is teaching that we always reap in our *physical life* what we have been sowing in our *mental life*—if not immediately, then eventually. This is especially true of viewing pornography. The seeds of those thoughts and fantasies may not be harvested overnight. The physical sin may not come for months, or even years. Because no lightning strikes and no angelic trumpets announce their sin, the viewer feels he can cover it up without anyone knowing. But who could deny that *physical* adultery is always preceded by *mental* adultery? Sooner or later, we always reap (act out) in our physical life what we have been sowing in our mental and emotional life.

Carrot seeds always produce carrots, just as radish seeds always produce radishes. It is inevitable, because we always reap as we sow. When we choose to inflame our passions by juggling the hot coals of pornography, for example, those indelible seeds that have been so carefully nourished cannot grow into anything else but a harvest of filthy, compelling thoughts and wicked deeds as we grow numb to consequences and then act out the things we have locked in our minds with the many sessions of pornographic fantasy.

"CAN A MAN TAKE FIRE IN HIS BOSOM, AND HIS CLOTHES NOT BE BURNED?"

Some will disagree because they have looked at pornography or indulged lustful thoughts without acting them out physically. This is exactly how Satan lures us deeper and deeper into the mental and emotional habit patterns that eventually reap the harvest of sexual sins such as masturbation and adultery.

In our first series of yielding to temptation, we create a vulnerability to give in to future temptations. That vulnerability is both cumulative and progressive, so that every compromise makes the next one easier. No one can quench the flames of desire while continuing to put wood on the fire. This is especially true of sexual sin, which feeds upon itself in such a way that the hunger is never satisfied, but grows stronger and more demanding for additional indulgence. Temporary thrills of illicit sexual pleasures can quickly evolve into an unexpected and uncontrollable monster that demands more and more of the person's time and emotion.

President Kimball warned, "*Sin is intensely habit-forming,*" and "as the transgressor moves deeper and deeper in his sin, and the error is entrenched more deeply and the will to change is weakened, it becomes increasingly nearer hopeless and he skids down and down until either he *does not want* to climb back up or he has *lost the power* to do so."[4]

"CAN A MAN TAKE FIRE IN HIS BOSOM, AND HIS CLOTHES NOT BE BURNED?"

The most immediate and devastating consequence of indulging the fires of illegitimate passion is the loss of the Lord's Spirit, and to lose the Spirit is to lose our battles. Because our mortal brains simply cannot run two programs at the same time, when we entertain lustful thoughts, pornographic images, and fantasies, we automatically drive the Spirit away. Thus, "he that looketh upon a woman to lust after her *shall* deny the faith, and *shall not have the Spirit*; and if he repents not he *shall* be cast out" (D&C 42:23; emphasis added). Does using the word *shall* three times in the same sentence leave any room for doubt? "And verily I say unto you, as I have said before, he that looketh on a woman to lust after her, or if any shall commit adultery in their hearts, they *shall not have the Spirit*, but shall deny the faith and shall fear" (D&C 63:16; emphasis added). Consider this sobering warning from Elder Joseph B. Wirthlin: "Every *ounce* of pornography and immoral entertainment will cause you to lose a *pound* of spirituality. And it will only take a few ounces of immorality to cause you to lose all of your spiritual strength, for the Lord's spirit will not dwell in an unclean temple."[5]

The best way to avoid being burned by the hot fires of immorality is to honor the sacramental covenant to remember Christ in our daily activities, to seek the Spirit by frequent prayer and scripture study, and to anticipate and avoid tempting circumstances that could arouse unworthy passions. "O that they were wise . . . [and] that they *would consider* their latter end!" (Deuteronomy 32:29; emphasis added). One of the most important things to "consider" as we make choices is to look past the immediacy of present circumstances to the long-range consequences. "A prudent man foreseeth [anticipates] the evil, and hideth [prepares] himself: but the simple pass on, and are punished" (Proverbs 22:3). Look past today, the Lord pleads, and walk "uprightly before me, *considering the end of your salvation*" (D&C 46:7; emphasis added).

"CAN A MAN TAKE FIRE IN HIS BOSOM, AND HIS CLOTHES NOT BE BURNED?

Conclusion: How could applying the principles taught by this chapter's question help you to feel better about yourself, improve your relationship with the Lord, and lead you to greater feelings of happiness and peace?

NOTES

1. "Privileges and Responsibilities of Sisters," *Ensign*, November 1978, 105; emphasis added.
2. "Struggle for the Soul," *New Era*, March 1984, 38.
3. "What the Bible Says About Sex," *Reader's Digest*, May 1970, 118, as quoted by Spencer W. Kimball, "Guidelines to Carry Forth the Work of God in Cleanliness," *Ensign*, May 1974, 7–8; emphasis added.
4. *The Miracle of Forgiveness*, 117; emphasis added.
5. "Little Things Count," *New Era*, May 1988, 7; emphasis added.

CHAPTER TWENTY-FOUR

CAN ANY HIDE HIMSELF IN SECRET PLACES THAT I SHALL NOT SEE HIM?

Can any hide himself in secret places that I shall not see him? saith the Lord. Do not I fill heaven and earth? saith the Lord. (Jeremiah 23:24)

THE ANSWER TO this important question is an emphatic no, for "the eyes of the Lord are in every place, beholding the evil and the good" (Proverbs 15:3). Yet it is so easy to become preoccupied with our day-to-day affairs that we often forget how watchful God and His angels are as they record not only our actions, but also our every word, thought, and intent (see Matthew 12:36; Alma 12:14; D&C 18:38; 88:109). The relevance of this question is the inescapable influence our perception of its answer has on our daily choices. For example, out of a thousand crimes or sins, how many would be eliminated if the person choosing the wrong were consciously aware of being watched at that precise moment by an authority that would then hold them accountable? "But behold, ye cannot hide your crimes from God; and except ye repent they will stand as a testimony against you at the last day" (Alma 39:8).

One of Satan's greatest lures into sin is his lie that we can get away with it if we do it in secret, unseen by our fellow man. But the scriptures teach that there is no such thing as a secret sin, "for there is nothing covered, that shall not be revealed; and hid, that shall not be known" (Matthew 10:26), and "*nothing* is secret, that shall not be made manifest; neither any thing hid, that shall not be known and come abroad" (Luke 8:17; emphasis added).

"CAN ANY HIDE HIMSELF IN SECRET PLACES THAT I SHALL NOT SEE HIM?"

Another enticement used by Satan is the illusion that we can sin safely and undetected if we do it at night, under the cover of darkness, as if the Lord wouldn't notice because He is asleep. But the Lord doesn't keep office hours or go off duty for a break, for "he that keepeth Israel shall neither slumber nor sleep" (Psalm 121:4) and "there is no darkness . . . where the workers of iniquity may hide themselves" (Job 34:22). Thus, "if I say, Surely the darkness shall cover me; even the night shall be light about me. Yea, the darkness and the light are both alike to thee" (Psalm 139:11–12).

Because a person no longer has to risk their reputation with the fear of being seen renting or buying pornography, the satanic illusion of private, secret, unnoticed sin is one of the major factors in the rapidly spreading epidemic of addiction to cable, satellite, and Internet pornography. Right in the privacy of our own homes, with a few easy clicks of a TV remote or computer mouse, we can now have instant access to pornographic filth that would have dumbfounded our parents less than a generation ago.

But who would dare to access such damaging images if they could only remember that the Savior is right there in the room with them, His heart breaking as He looks at the same TV or computer screen, for He has assured us that not only are "his eyes are upon the ways of man" (Job 34:21), but also that "[he is] in your midst and ye cannot see [him]" (D&C 38:7). As President Kimball warned, "There are no corners so dark, no deserts so uninhabited, no canyons so remote, no automobiles so hidden, no homes so tight and shut but that the all-seeing one can penetrate and observe."[1] And the Lord said, "For mine eyes are upon all their ways: they are not hid from my face, neither is their iniquity hid from mine eyes" (Jeremiah 16:17).

"CAN ANY HIDE HIMSELF IN SECRET PLACES THAT I SHALL NOT SEE HIM?"

As soon as we forget that God is watching our daily lives, we also forget that there are consequences to our choices. The longer we persist in the delusion that our sins won't count if they are not observed, the worse our degeneracy becomes because every choice and action plants within our cells the inclination to repeat the action until it becomes a habitual part of our character and preferences. Moses warned that if you have sinned, you can "be sure your sin will find you out" (Numbers 32:23). Similarly, Paul warned, "Neither is there any creature that is not manifest in his sight: *but all things are naked and opened unto the eyes of him with whom we have to do*" (Hebrews 4:13; emphasis added).

For the deliberately sinful person, such scriptures strike terror into a guilty conscience—as they should. But the very same verses bring hope and encouragement to those who are trying to live righteously. As Elder Horacio A. Tenorio said, "Our Heavenly Father loves us dearly and watches over us in all our needs and cares, following us through life step by step."[2]

The Lord's concerned and attentive watchfulness over His children has been one of the major themes throughout all of scripture. For example, attempting to persuade a Lamanite king that the Great Spirit he worshiped not only "created all things which are in heaven and in the earth" but also maintains a constant, watchful care over His children, the great missionary Ammon told King Lamoni:

> The heavens is a place where God dwells and all his holy angels.
> And king Lamoni said: Is it above the earth?
> And Ammon said: Yea, and *he looketh down upon all the children of men; and he knows all the thoughts and intents of the heart.* (Alma 18:30–32; emphasis added)

Jesus once attempted to teach us how constant and detailed Father's watchfulness is by stating that not even a lowly sparrow could fall to the ground without His notice. And if that assurance was not conclusive, He went on to say that God knows so much about each individual that even "the very hairs of your head are all numbered" (Matthew 10:29–30). Remembering that God is ever mindful of us and watching us not only day by day, but also deed by deed and choice by choice will help us ignore Satan's enticing lie that we can somehow escape the consequences of sins we attempt to hide in secrecy.

Remembering Christ and His loving attention to our daily activities is so important that He has given us the ordinance of the sacrament to be repeated once every seven days. It is with the sacrament that we are reminded of the importance of focusing our daily attention on the Savior and, renew our promise to do so. By sincerely participating in this ordinance, we not only witness to the Father that we are "willing to take upon [us] the name" of Christ, but also that we will try to *always remember him and keep his commandments*" (D&C 20:77; emphasis added).

The key to keeping the commandments consistently and faithfully is the promise we receive for *remembering* him, the promise that for so doing, we "may always have his Spirit to be with [us]" (D&C 20:77). And isn't that exactly what we all need to sustain us if we are to know Him personally, obey Him, and feel close to Him? When remembering comes first, the obedience will follow almost automatically.

"CAN ANY HIDE HIMSELF IN SECRET PLACES THAT I SHALL NOT SEE HIM?"

Conclusion: How could applying the principles taught by this chapter's question help you to feel better about yourself, improve your relationship with the Lord, and lead you to greater feelings of happiness and peace?

NOTES

1. *The Miracle of Forgiveness*, 110.
2. "Teachings of a Loving Father," *Ensign*, May 1990, 79.

CHAPTER TWENTY-FIVE

THEREFORE, WHAT MANNER OF MEN OUGHT YE TO BE?

Therefore, what manner of men ought ye to be? Verily I say unto you, even as I am. (3 Nephi 27:27)

IN THE BEGINNING of this mortal world God created man in His own image *physically*. However, the creative process is not finished. Our challenge during mortality is to partner with God to create ourselves in His image spiritually, morally, mentally, emotionally, behaviorally, and in every other way so that "as we have borne the image of the earthy, we shall also bear the image of the heavenly" (1 Corinthians 15:49).

We go to college to become a lawyer, a doctor, an engineer, a nurse, and so forth. We come to this earth school to learn to become like Christ and Heavenly Father. "Behold," said Christ, "I am the light; I have set an example for you" (3 Nephi 18:16). "Therefore, what manner of men ought ye to be?" (3 Nephi 27:27). His answer has compelling implications for the manner in which we must use our time and our bodies: "Verily I say unto you, *even as I am*" (3 Nephi 27:27; emphasis added). For us, Shakespeare's famous question, "To be, or not to be," should be rephrased: "To be like Christ, or not to be like Christ? That is the all important question."

Peter said, "Christ also suffered for us, *leaving us an example*, that ye should follow his steps" (1 Peter 2:21; emphasis added). Jesus came to reveal and demonstrate the kind of being God is, as well as to set the standard that we are expected to meet if we wish to dwell with Him throughout eternity. As Truman Madsen said, "Here is an attempt to illustrate this magnificent Mormon insight: that Christ is both the revelation of God as he is and the revelation of man as he may become."[1]

Alma asked, "Have ye received his image in your countenances? Have ye experienced this mighty change in your hearts?" (Alma 5:14). We would do well to ask ourselves if we have also received his image in our attitudes, in our personalities, values, trustworthiness, and service. How well are we doing in following His example and striving to be what the Savior exemplified? Christ said, "My sheep hear my voice . . . and *they follow me*" (John 10:27; emphasis added). Not only are we to follow His example in the kind of person we are to be, but also in doing the things that He did in service to others, "for the works which ye have seen me do that shall ye also do" (3 Nephi 27:21). "Wherefore, follow me, and do the things which ye have seen me do" (2 Nephi 31:12).

"THEREFORE, WHAT MANNER OF MEN OUGHT YE TO BE?"

If we are really committed to the celestial kingdom, then following Christ's example is not a choice, for "unless a man shall endure to the end, in following the example of the Son of the living God, he cannot be saved" (2 Nephi 31:16). Yet, from the ancient tower of Babel to modern positive thinking and humanism, fallen men have been concocting substitute schemes for finding their way back to heaven. Countless religions and philosophies have been devised to lift men above the animal plane toward a higher spirituality. Christ's message is, "I am the way" back to the Father, and "no man cometh unto the Father, but by me" (John 14:6; emphasis added). Indeed, it is so important for us to focus on His example that He said, "I give unto you this commandment—that no man shall come unto the Father but by me or by my word, which is my law, saith the Lord" (D&C 132:12).

"THEREFORE, WHAT MANNER OF MEN OUGHT YE TO BE?"

When the scriptures teach that "Christ is the *end of the law* for righteousness to everyone that believeth" (Romans 10:4; emphasis added), they mean that He ended the law of Moses, but also that He is the *ultimate example* to follow. As Peter expressed it, through the example provided by Christ, the Lord "hath given unto us all things that pertain unto life and godliness, through the knowledge [example] of him that hath called us to glory and virtue" (2 Peter 1:3). In other words, there is nothing we need to *know*, nothing we need to *do* or *become* that has not been revealed and exemplified in the example of Christ's character and life. He is not just a good example; He is *the example* of all that we need to become to dwell with our Father in Heaven. As Elder Bernard P. Brockbank said, "The answers to knowing God the Eternal Father are found in and through Jesus Christ. . . . In order to know God the Eternal Father, we must receive that knowledge . . . through Jesus Christ, who is the mediator between God and man."[2]

"Remember, remember," pled Helaman, "that it is upon the rock of our Redeemer, who is Christ, the Son of God, that ye must build your foundation" (Helaman 5:12). The apostle John also emphasized the importance of making the Savior the example and foundation of our life when He said, "He that hath the Son hath life; and he that hath not the Son of God hath not life" (1 John 5:12). This could be reworded to say, "He that follows and emulates the example of the Son has a happy and successful spiritual life, while he that does not emulate the Savior has an empty and unfulfilled life." How often we cheat ourselves by trying to choose something in between.

John was telling us that every success or failure in life, every situation that lifts us or that pulls us down is related to the degree to which we follow Christ's example. As Vaughn J. Featherstone of the First Quorum of Seventy said, "Number one on our agenda, above all else, is faith in Christ. . . . Whenever we find problems in the Church, we usually find them under one of two umbrellas or canopies, either transgression or lack of faith in Christ."[3]

"Therefore, what manner of men ought ye to be? I say unto you, even as I am," and therefore, "I would that ye should be perfect even as I, or your Father who is in heaven is perfect" (3 Nephi 12:48). The idea that we could ever become as perfect as God is stunning, but through the power of the Atonement it will someday be possible. As we sincerely seek to follow the Savior's example, and as we accept the sanctifying effect of His Atonement and priesthood ordinances into our life, we become recipients of "exceeding great and precious promises: that by these [we] might *be partakers of the divine nature*" (2 Peter 1:4; emphasis added).

"Partaking of His divine nature" means that we have aligned our personality and actions so closely with His that we become "partakers of his holiness" (Hebrews 12:10) and "that we may be purified even as he is pure" (Moroni 7:48). Having thus partaken of His divine nature by following His example, the time will come when we will be able to "stand blameless before God at the last day" (D&C 4:2; also 3 Nephi 27:20). As Mormon said, "All who are true followers of his Son, Jesus Christ . . . may become the sons of God; that when he shall appear *we shall be like him* . . . [and that] we may have this hope; that we may be purified even as he is pure" (Moroni 7:48; emphasis added; also 1 John 3:2; 4:17). And in 2 Corinthians 7:1, it says, "Having therefore these promises, dearly beloved, let us cleanse ourselves from all filthiness of the flesh and spirit, perfecting holiness in the fear of God."

Learning to follow the Savior's example as we overcome the desires of the natural man is not easy and, in most cases, is not achieved quickly. Developing spiritual maturity takes time, determination, and persistence. It is not an event but a lifelong process. Thus Christ has said, "Ye must *practise* virtue and holiness before me continually" (D&C 46:33; emphasis added). The word *practise* shows that God is allowing us time to learn and grow and that we should "continue in patience until [we] are perfected" (D&C 67:13). Rather than feeling discouraged by shortcomings, we should try, like Paul, to remember that even though there is a long way to go, we must ever "press toward the mark for the prize of the high calling of God in Christ Jesus" (Philippians 3:14), and "run with patience the race that is set before us" (Hebrews 12:1).

Following Christ's example until we become like Him would be an incredibly unreachable goal for fallen mankind if we were left to achieve it by our abilities and merits alone. But with Christ's grace to expand and magnify our best efforts, it is achievable for every sincere disciple because Jesus is not only the *example* for what we are to become, but is also the *source* of the grace and strength we need to become like Him. By cooperating with Him, we make it possible for Him to "change our vile body, that it may be fashioned like unto his glorious body, according to the working whereby he is able even to subdue all things unto himself" (Philippians 3:21; also 2 Corinthians 3:18).

"I am the Way," the Savior tells those who hope to find the means, the way to create heaven. *Only in him can any man find the strength, the power, and the ability to live a godly life.* . . . Only in Christ is there power to transform the human mind and the human heart. . . . Only in Jesus Christ can any man learn the truth of what he is and how he can be changed from what he is to do the good for which he hopes.[4]

"THEREFORE, WHAT MANNER OF MEN OUGHT YE TO BE?"

In closing this chapter and this book, let us consider some of the rewards promised those who earnestly persist in following the example of Christ, and who, through His grace and Atonement, fulfill the purpose of their mortal probation by becoming like Him. To begin with, "he that is a faithful and wise steward shall *inherit all things*" (D&C 78:22; emphasis added) as "heirs of God, and *joint-heirs with Christ*; if so be that we suffer with him, that we may be also *glorified together*" (Romans 8:17; emphasis added). As Christ promised, "To him that overcometh will I grant to *sit with me in my throne*, even as I also overcame, and am set down with my Father in his throne" (Revelation 3:21; emphasis added).

> And they shall pass by the angels, and the gods, which are set there, to their exaltation and glory in all things. . . .
> And shall inherit thrones, kingdoms, principalities, and powers, dominions, all heights and depths. (D&C 132:19)

"The disciple is not above his master," said Christ, "but every one that is perfect *shall be as* his master" (Luke 6:40; emphasis added). Thus, "if you keep my commandments you shall receive of [the Father's] fulness, and be glorified in me as I am in the Father" (D&C 93:20). As we complete this mortal probation and graduate into exaltation, "The saints shall be filled with his glory, and receive their inheritance and *be made equal with him*" (D&C 88:107; emphasis added). And "then shall they be gods, because they have no end . . . [and] because they have all power, and the angels are subject unto them" (D&C 132:20). These concepts were beautifully summarized in this quote:

> The key to the door to the way of righteousness, then, is the knowledge of who and what Jesus Christ is. . . .
> Knowing what he *is*, we can know what the fulness of righteousness is. Knowing what he *did*, we can see what we must do to become righteous as he is. . . .
> It follows that our whole spiritual endeavor should be focused on emulating the Master. Mere external observance—church attendance, observing the laws of tithing, Word of Wisdom, and so on—are only the beginning; they do not fulfill the requirement. Though it is not easy, we are required to so school ourselves to make habitual in our lives the

kind of response Jesus made to his life situations and to act in keeping with such responses. To do this we will need to meet our own life situations and problems with questions such as, "How would Jesus feel?"[5]

"THEREFORE, WHAT MANNER OF MEN OUGHT YE TO BE?"

The ultimate reward of exaltation, however, goes beyond perfection and equality with God into a realm of perfect joy and fulfillment. "At [His] right hand there are pleasures for evermore," and "in [His] presence is fulness of joy" (Psalm 16:11). "And for this cause," promised the Savior, "ye shall have fulness of joy; and ye shall sit down in the kingdom of my Father; yea, *your joy shall be full,* even as the Father hath given me fulness of joy; *and ye shall be even as I am*" (3 Nephi 28:10; emphasis added).

I believe that sincere consideration and response to the meaning and message of each of the questions discussed in this book will provide significant stepping stones in our quest to become like the Savior, as well as a significant increase in our feelings of happiness, self-acceptance, and fellowship with deity.

"THEREFORE, WHAT MANNER OF MEN OUGHT YE TO BE?"

Conclusion: Do you believe that applying the principles taught by this chapter's question, along with all the previous chapters' questions, will help you to feel better about yourself, improve your relationship with the Lord, friends, and family, and lead you to greater feelings of happiness and peace?

I hope they will do that for you—as they have for me.

NOTES

1. Truman G. Madsen, *Christ and the Inner Life*, 2nd ed. (Salt Lake City: Bookcraft, 1978), 1.
2. "Knowing God," *Ensign*, July 1972, 121.
3. "The Torchbearer," *BYU Devotional Speeches of the Year* (Provo, Utah: Brigham Young University Press, 1982–83), 145.
4. *In His Footsteps Today*, 4; emphasis added.
5. *In His Footsteps Today*, 5–7.

ABOUT THE AUTHOR

STEVEN A. CRAMER is the pen name for Gerald Curtis, author of more than a dozen books and talk tapes.

Since the release of his first book, *The Worth of a Soul*, in 1980, he has sold more than a quarter million books and tapes, helping people rise from the defeat of weaknesses, bad habits, and addictions, into the loving arms of the Savior, by learning to apply the Atonement of Jesus Christ in their lives.

Professionally, Steven worked for the United States Postal Service, the aerospace industry, and in sales. In the Church, he has served in a variety of positions, including as bishop and twice as a senior missionary with his wife, LoAnne Richardson. Steven now devotes the majority of his time to family history work. He and LoAnne have been married for over forty-eight years. They are the parents of nine children, and they have more than thirty grandchildren.